Invited on a bear hunting trip in Mississippi in 1902, USA President Theodore Roosevelt had failed to shoot anything, unlike most of the hunting party. His aides tracked down a bear, exhausted after being chased by hounds. They tied it to a tree and encouraged the President to shoot it. Roosevelt declined, feeling that it would be unsporting. 'Teddy's Bear' had arrived. The following day the story was re-enacted in a satirical cartoon in the Washington Post. And a potential embarrassment became the start of a success story.

Two New York shopkeepers, Rose and Morris Mitchom, had the idea to commemorate the event by manufacturing a stuffed baby bear, which they would call Teddy. President Roosevelt gave his blessing, and the bear soon began to be appear in every family home. Rose & Morris's small shop soon became the 'Ideal Novelty and Toy Company'. Sixty years later, the very first Teddy was pre-sented to Roosevelt's grandson by the son of the Mitchoms. Today the bear can be found in Washington's Smithsonian Museum, where, in 2012, he celebrated his 100th birthday.

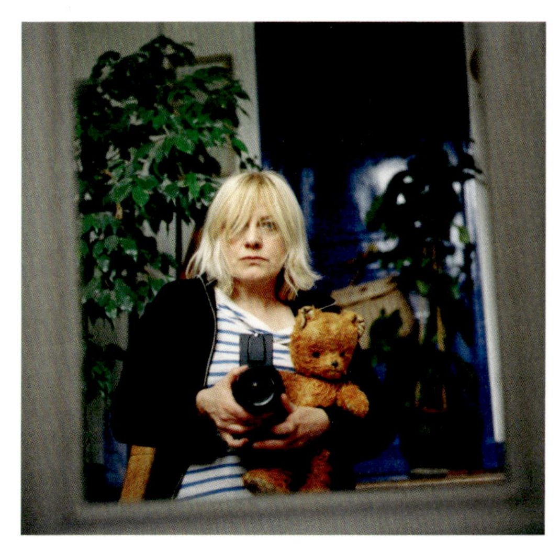

2004. The reunion.
Everything starts from here.

For Rosalie, Suzanne & Jean

a story of bears

sylvie huet

dewi lewis publishing

My mother didn't throw anything away.

This is the first sentence of *À la guerre comme à la guerre*, by Tomi Ungerer, whose teddy bear, Otto, appears in this book.

If only I could have said the same thing, but my mother threw mine away. Yet, because of this, when I rediscovered him 30 years later, I could imagine this book.

So, thank you.

1957 - 2004

Cocaine is nothing more
than a picture taken by
my father, which
follows me everywhere.

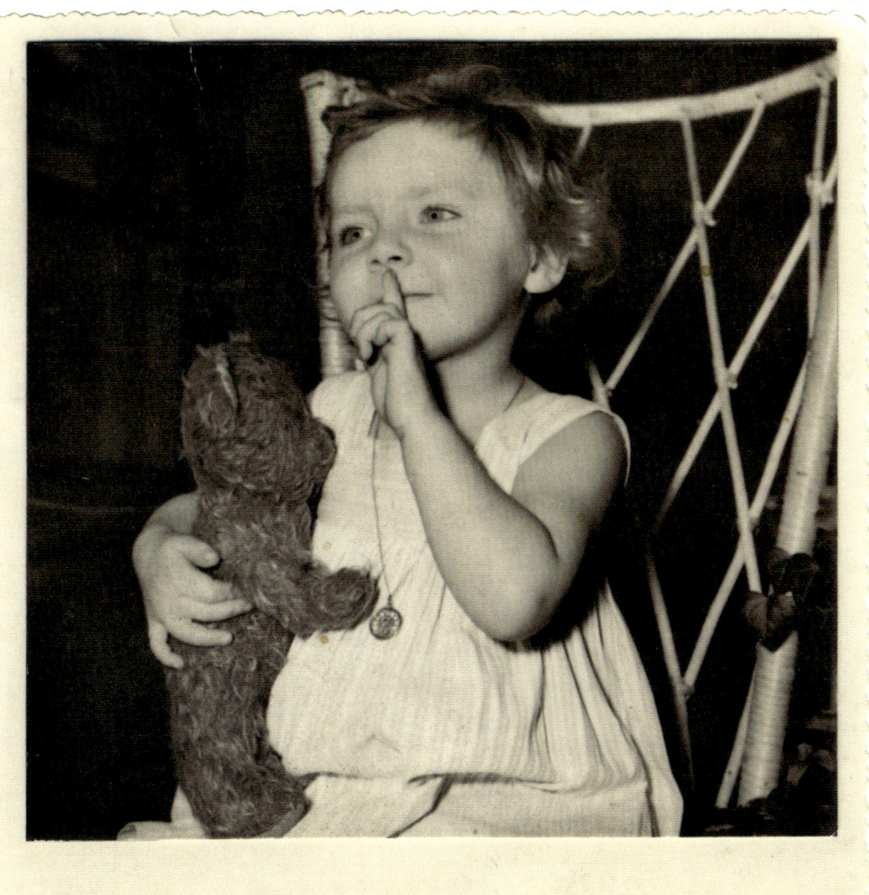

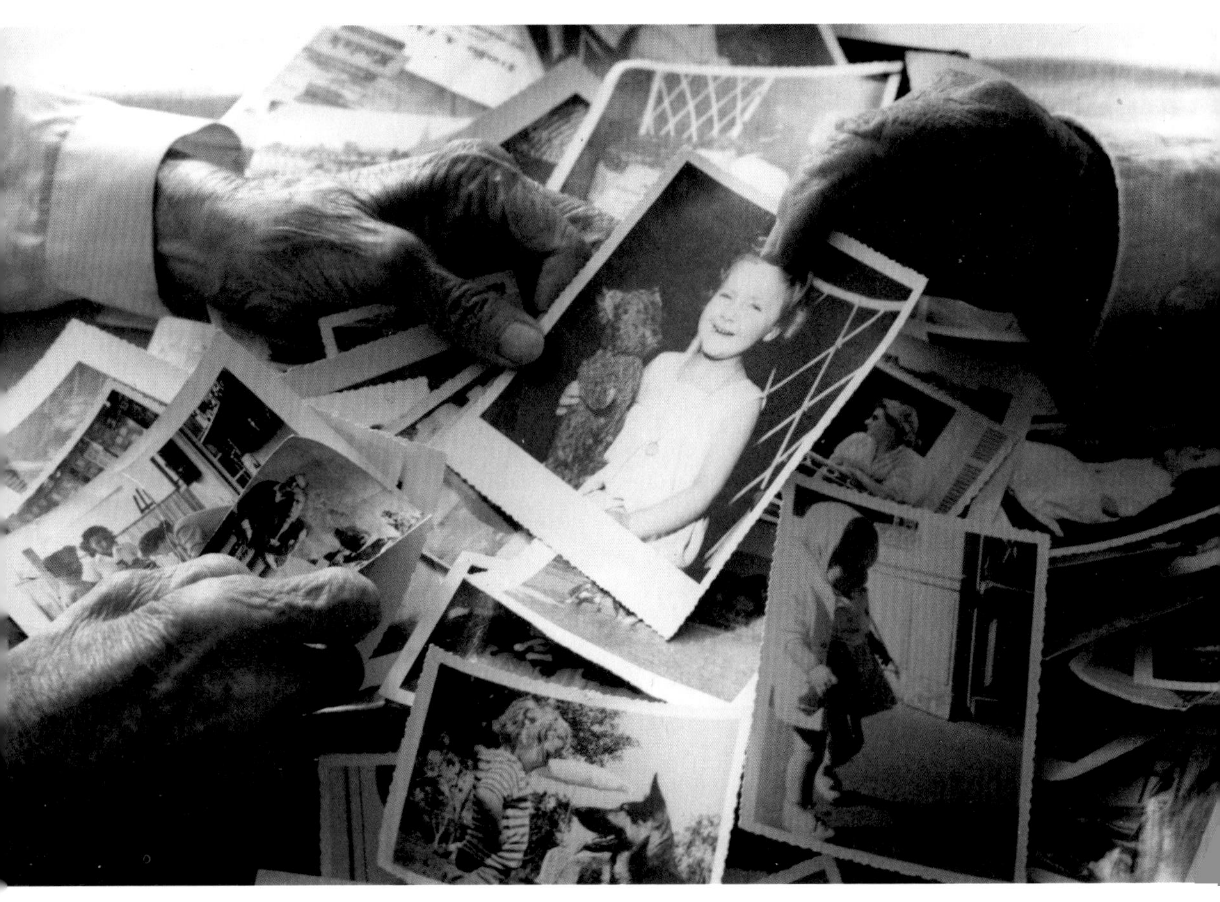

in the words of 'copain'…

One Sunday, in the flea market where I had been taken by an antique dealer, I noticed a woman staring at me from a distance. She looked dumbfounded. She came close, picked me up and squeezed me to her chest; not something that teddy bear collectors usually do. It reminded me of how, many years ago, in this same town, a little girl had held me when she was sad.

Later, her mother got rid of me – nothing I could do about it. Was it her? The little girl? I couldn't recognise her, people change too quickly. When she asked "how much?" the dealer replied "€150… it's a very sought after bear." He couldn't have known exactly how sought after.

A short while later I was back in my old home. Two pairs of eyes looked me up and down. "Is it really him?" Sylvie's parents were convinced that I was an imposter until, having searched through the boxes of childhood photographs, they recognised certain distinguishing features that could only belong to me. They couldn't ignore the evidence.

Afraid of losing me again, Sylvie took me home to her house in Paris.

This is my story and, because of my story, other people have told me theirs. They live with the bears of their childhood, their confidants, their inspiration, and they have introduced me to them. These beloved bears come from all walks of life and from every corner of the world. Distant memories are triggered, sometimes serious, often joyous.

The teddy bear
who belonged to
Marianne Salmine

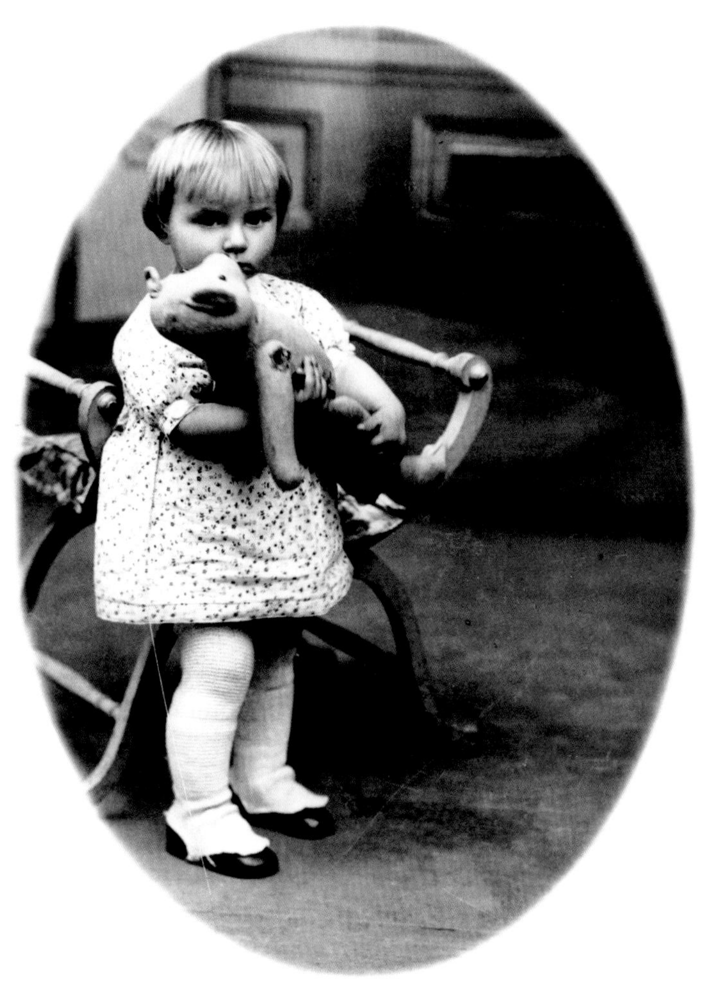

I remember I used to sleep with my Mother under the roofs. There was a very small room that was ours. We reached it by a staircase, very impressive like most vertical attic or cellar staircases with small, narrow steps. So my Mother used to put me to bed with her when she had finished work, which was sometimes very late. I often used to sleep in a corner, on the floor. I still can see myself at the top of the stairs when I woke up; I think I was calling my Mother.

This photo, which I had forgotten, is the only trace of my teddy bear, but I feel as if he had never left me.

Look at him closely! He has the look of teddy bears of the period. He was hard, rough, 'cafe-au-lait' coloured with darker ears. He was stuffed with horse hair and he was my bear. I loved him.

This bear, I believe, is my first real despair. Above all, I remember the day when I woke up and could no longer find my teddy bear. My mother had taken him from me while I was asleep and thrown him away because in her opinion he was...

Too old? Too dirty? too damaged! All of those!, and I screamed in despair at the top of this attic stairs.

Marianne

The Orphan
age: 98
belongs to:
Suzanne

In the port of Nantes, the old lady Suzanne, a widow, without children, died, entrusting the only family she had ever had to her neighbours across the hallway. It was Suzanne who had knitted his royal blue zip-up suit. The neighbours 'lent' me their lodger after having heard of my project but have never asked for him back. It is as if his story has started over again from that point. I've searched for a long time for a hallway in which to photograph Suzanne's orphan, a special place between two doors.

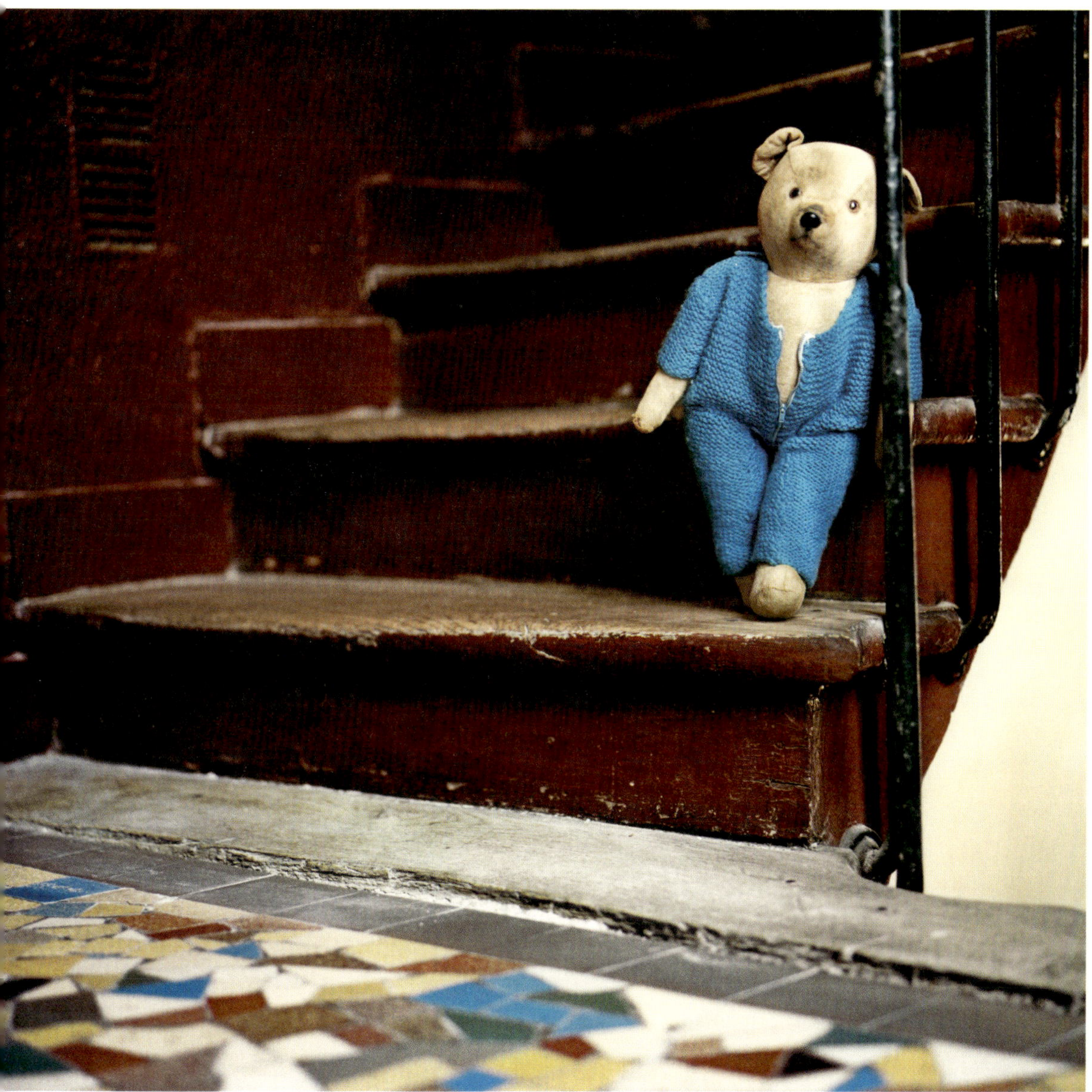

Tintin

age: 88

belongs to:

Elisabeth Lefebvre

My sister Bénédicte and I loved going to our grandparents in rue
Caulaincourt. My grandfather would show his papers and proudly tell
us that he was a citizen of the town of Montmartre. Every Sunday we
went to mass at Saint-Pierre de Montmartre, stopping, fascinated, to
watch the painters in the Place du Tertre. My grandmother, who had
been a seamstress for the famous couturier Jeanne Lanvin, would,
at our request, make costumes for Tintin. He belonged to our father
who was born in 1923. Grandmother kept this last trace of her only
son in my father's old bedroom, where he waited quietly for our visits.
When she left rue Caulaincourt after 96 years to return to Corrèze,
she asked me to clear out the apartment. Tintin had remained in a
box of souvenirs. One day, lifting an old cloth, I discovered his little
head. His sweet smile had been repaired several times with black
thread. My heart jumped for joy. My little sister and my father have
since passed away. Tintin is a joy to my grandchildren but he remains
firmly in my loving care.

Elisabeth Lefebvre

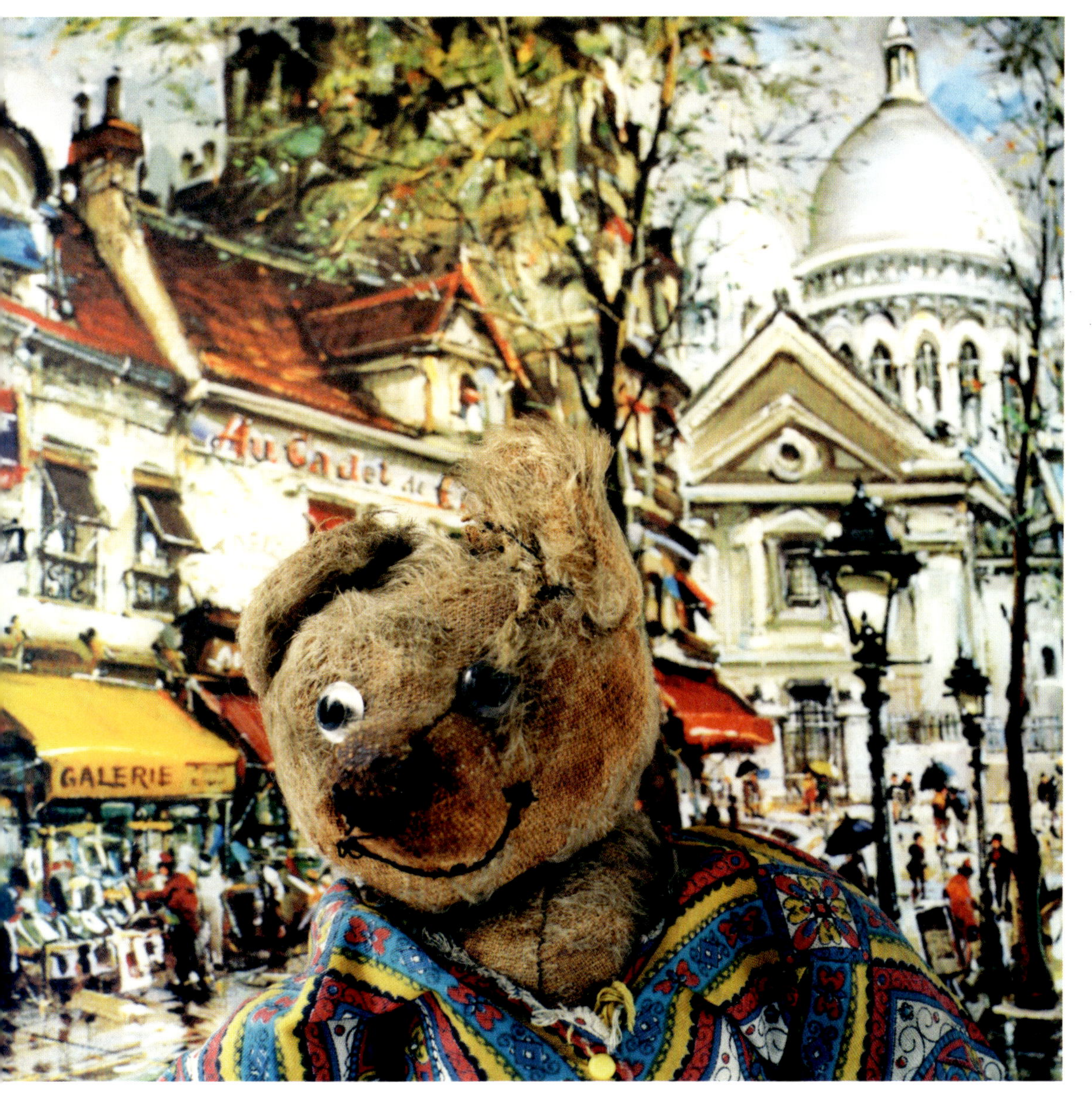

Michka
age: 54
belongs to:
Jean-Patrick Belloir

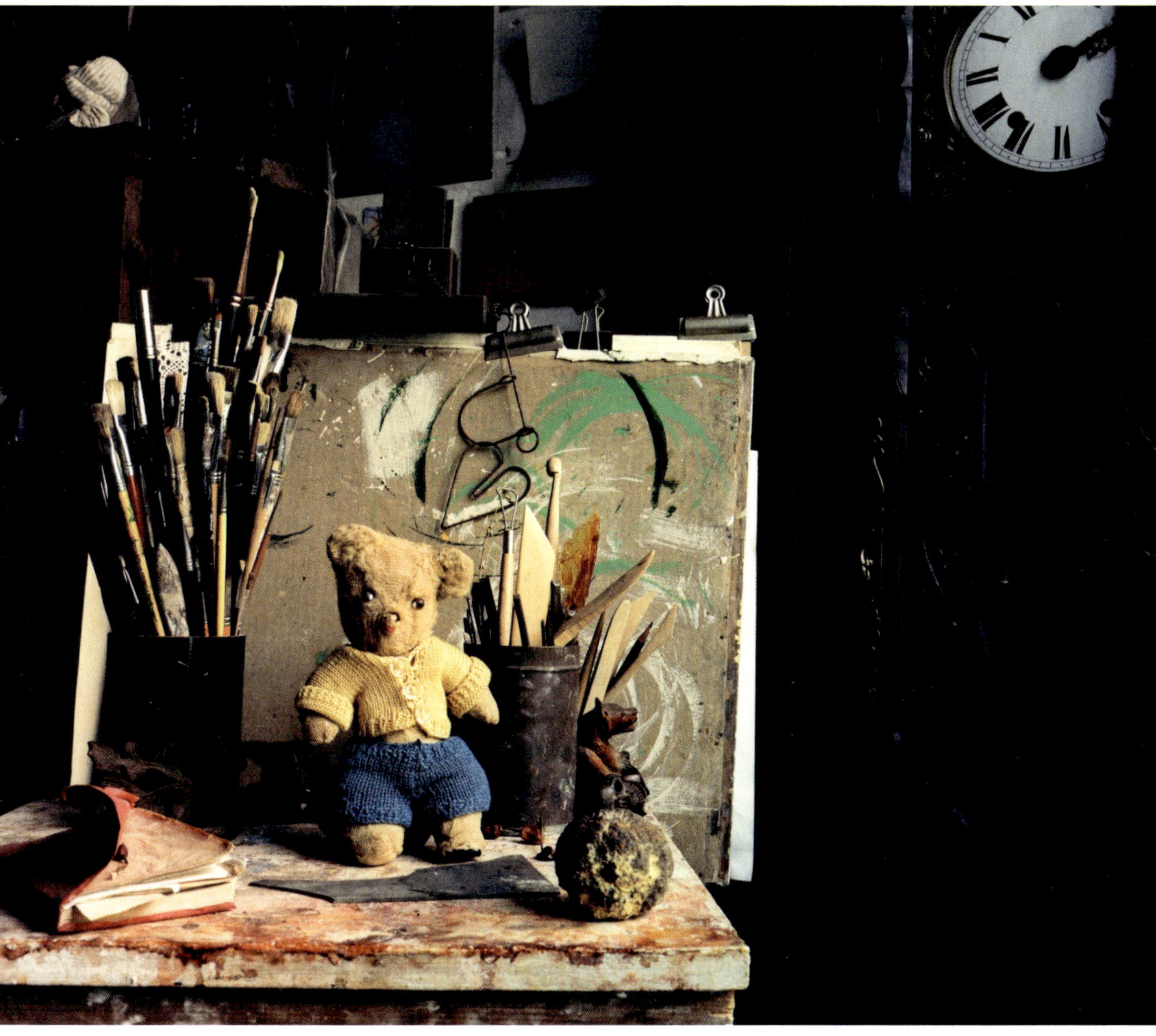

Michka, the eponymous hero of my favourite book, said farewell to his freedom on Christmas Eve 1959 by becoming my super-bear, my watchful eye, my alter ego.

Off camping? I would build him a house from cardboard. Winter sports? I would make him an igloo. To the seaside? His own small sailboat.

On the day of my seventh birthday I decided to cut his hair, thinking I could do it as my mother did mine; he became old very young.

Jean-Patrick Belloir

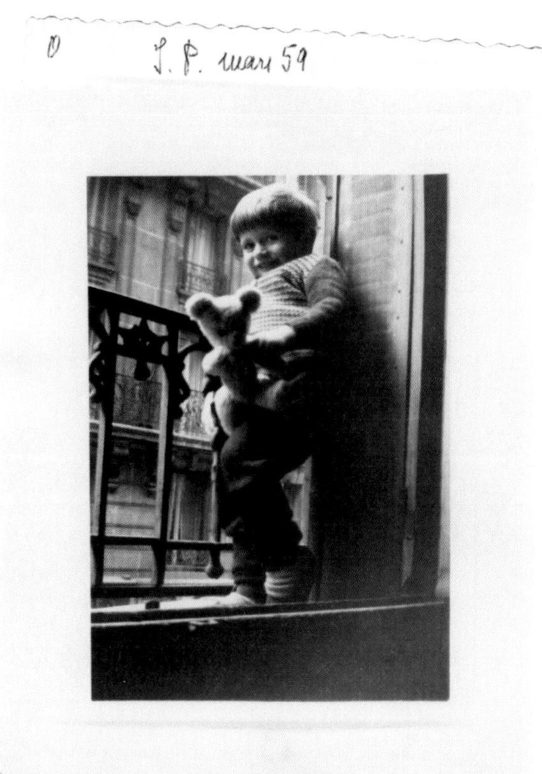

J. P. mars 59

Teddy
age: 60
belongs to:
Eva Kempinsky

Teddy came into my life when I was 5 years old. So that I could attend the holiday camp at Les Andelys I was placed in the care of my big brother. Before abandoning us to our sad fate, my parents revealed, as if by magic, a character in all his glory: Teddy. He quickly took his place in my life; a comforting confidant, he became my closest friend…

… I was 12 years old and Teddy was still my ally. Three days after arriving for a winter sports holiday, I had to return to Paris to keep my grandfather company. I was feeling miserable. I sorted out my things, but, for whatever reason, Teddy was left behind…

… One night, finally, I could hear my parents and brother coming back in the car. Perhaps this is a memory that I invented, but my brother had a guilty look. He gave me back a Teddy that was very different to the one that I had left with him: the one that he gave back to me had only one leg! An inquiry was conducted. He had used Teddy in a fight game as an attack weapon.

Today, I always have this wonderful friend, more than half a century old, near to me. His expression shows that he doesn't hold it against me that I exposed him to this violence or that I left without even kissing him goodbye. He always lets me know of his immense love, tinged however with a hint of reproach.

Eva Kempinsky

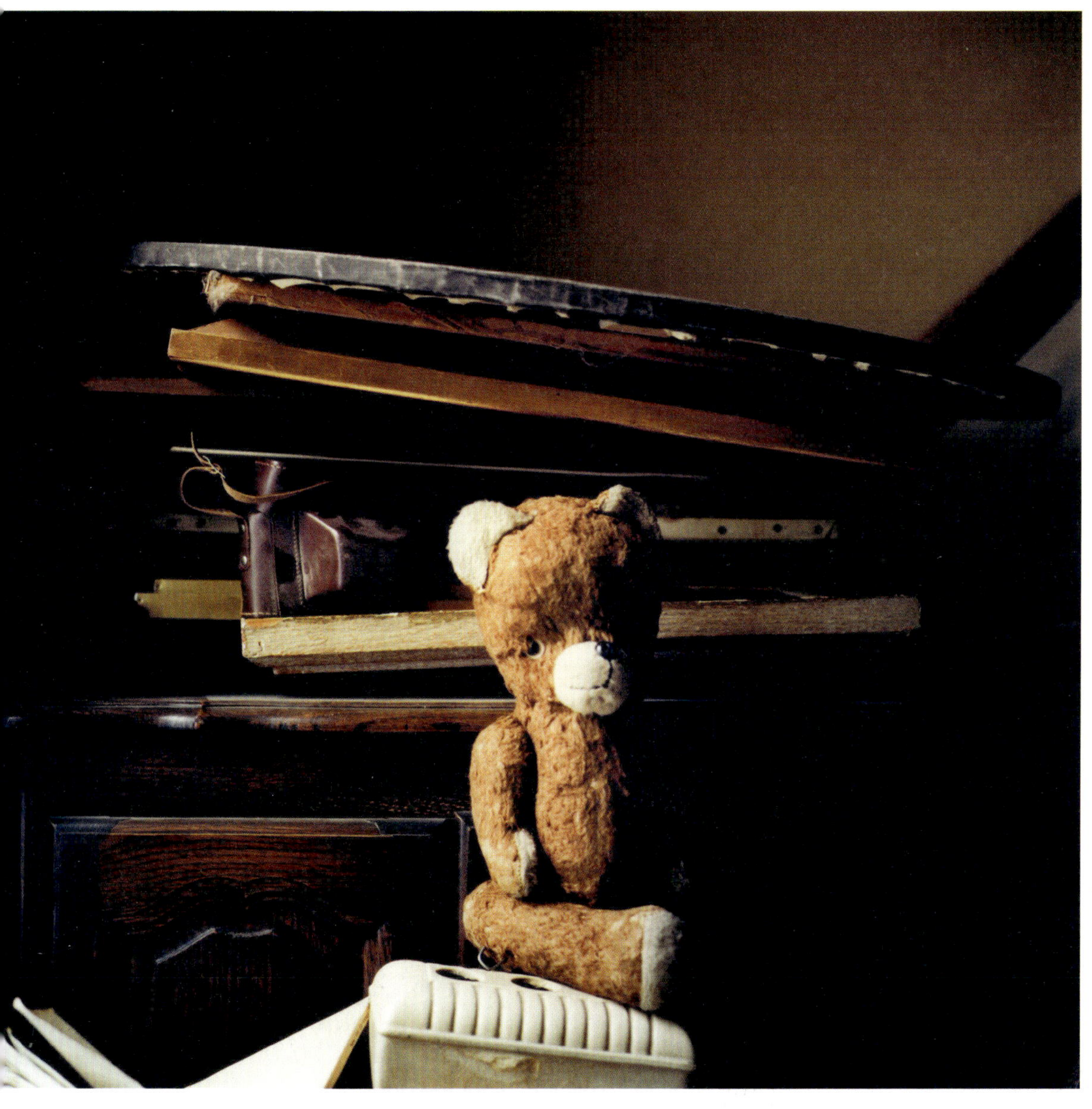

Rac
age: 81
belongs to:
Michel Caté

Rac, the sailor

Edouard Caté, a sea captain and indefatigable traveller, lived in Le Havre and was accustomed to take his cocker spaniel with him on his trips to the distant shores of Southern Africa. In 1933, to console his son Michel for his long absences, he gave him a stuffed toy that looked just like Rac.

In 1942, during the war, while the whole family was temporarily living on the 'St Basile', a cargo ship docked in Marseille, the real Rac attacked the toy dog. Time did the rest.

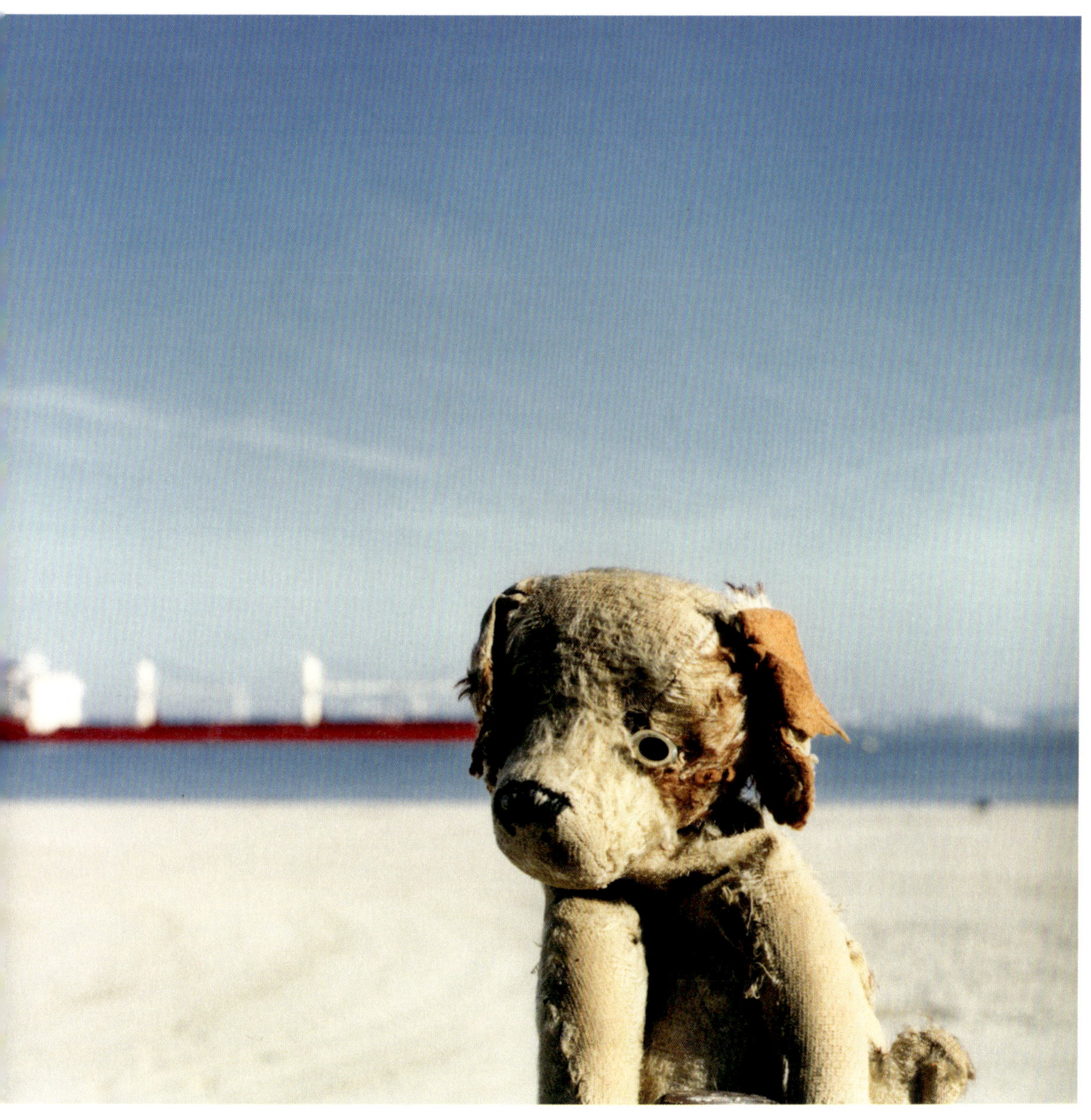

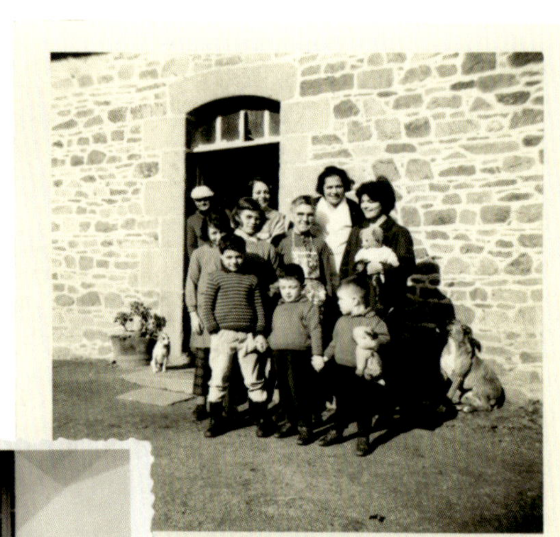

Rac with Hervé, Michel's son,
on the front row, right

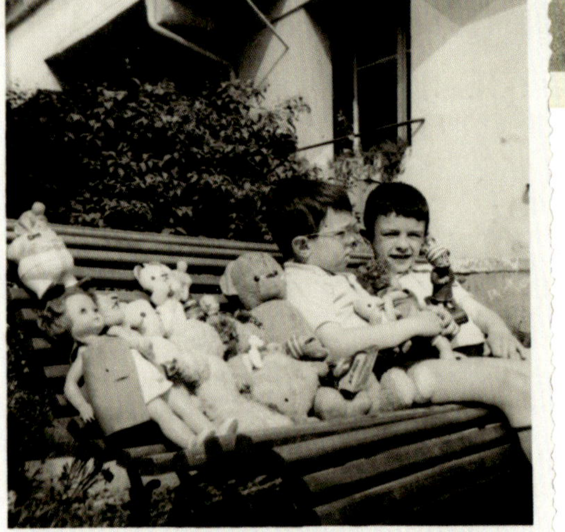

Hervé, Laurent, the band of 4 bears
and others... 1965

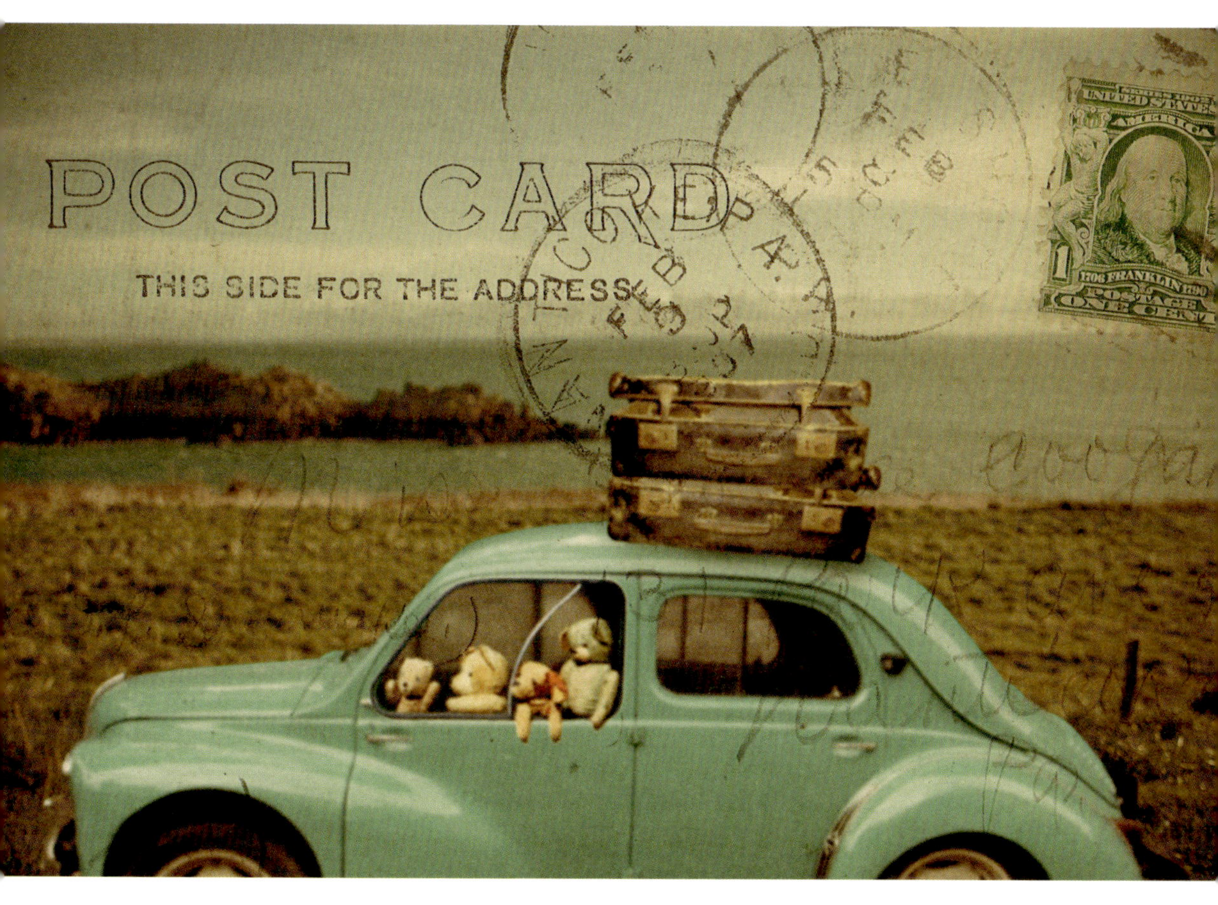

On the annual holiday to Brittany.
Rac, Tintin, Grousson & Teddy travel
together with Michel and his children.

Eddy - Bear

age : 62

be longs to:

Marie - Laure

I, 'Teddy bear', produced by
gentle and skilled hands, only
really came to life in 1945 when
I was given to a little girl who
called me Eddy Bear.
The two of us travelled extensively
before returning to our starting
point in Normandy.
                    Marie-Laure

Every year on All Saints Day, Marie-Laure lays flowers on the
doorstep of her family home. It is a ritual act to honour the house.
Rooted among the hundred-year-old oaks, it was destroyed by fire
and never rebuilt. It was a coincidence that the day of our meeting
fell on that same day.

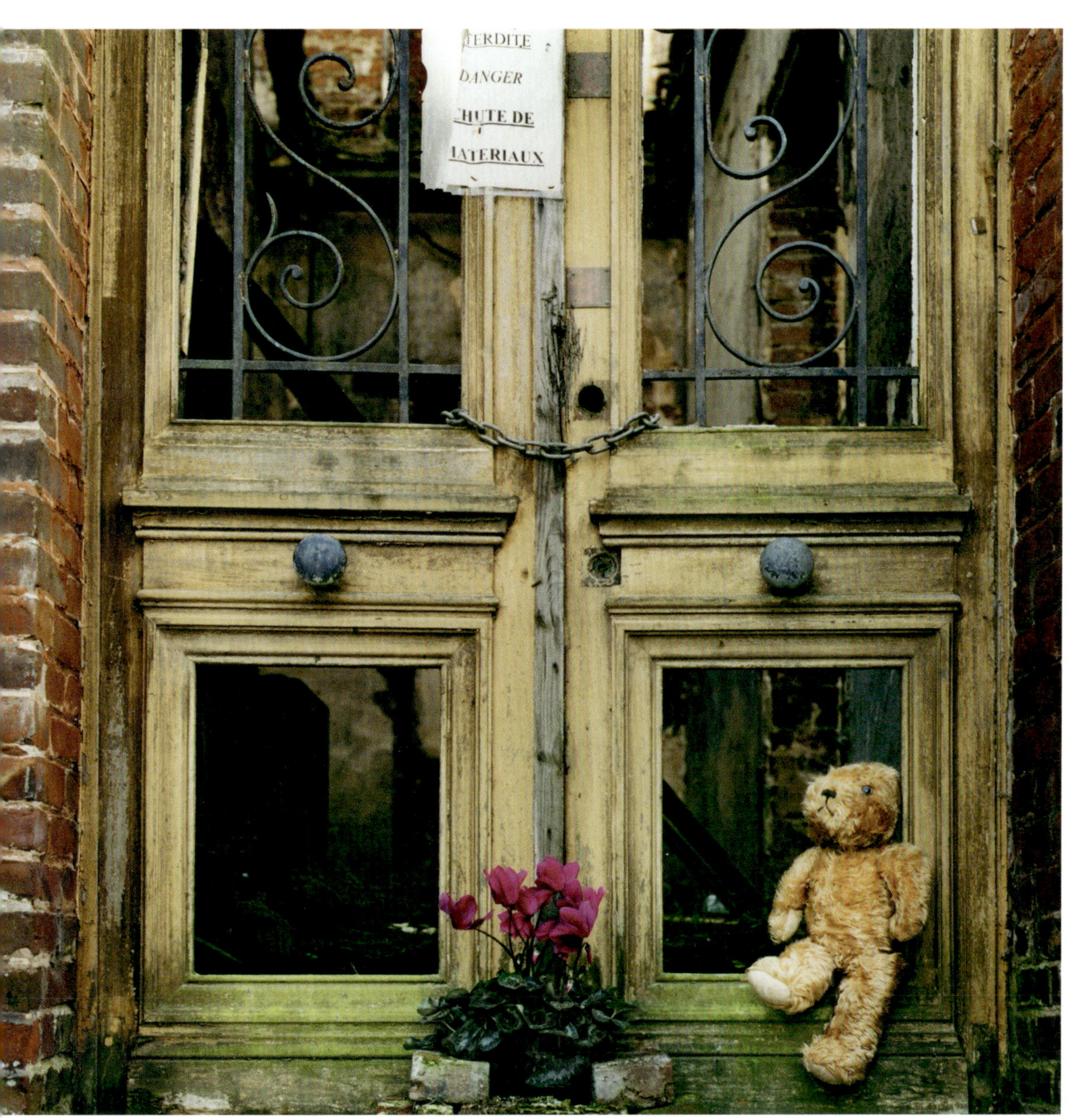

TERDITE
DANGER
HUTE DE
IATERIAUX

Teddy
age: 57
belongs to:
Berthe

Berthe lives alone. She is 97 years old when I talk to her about my project. She lived with her mother until her death at the age of 104. Berthe wants to entrust her teddy to me. It was a gift from her mother on her 40th birthday, but she won't talk about him! It would 'disturb her mother'. By becoming friends with the bear, I won over Berthe.

We talked for hours, sharing her whisky and the millefeuilles that I'd bought on the way to her home. We talked... of everything except the bear.

Berthe was buried in the cemetery at Saint-Denis in 2012 ... along with her bear, as she had wanted.

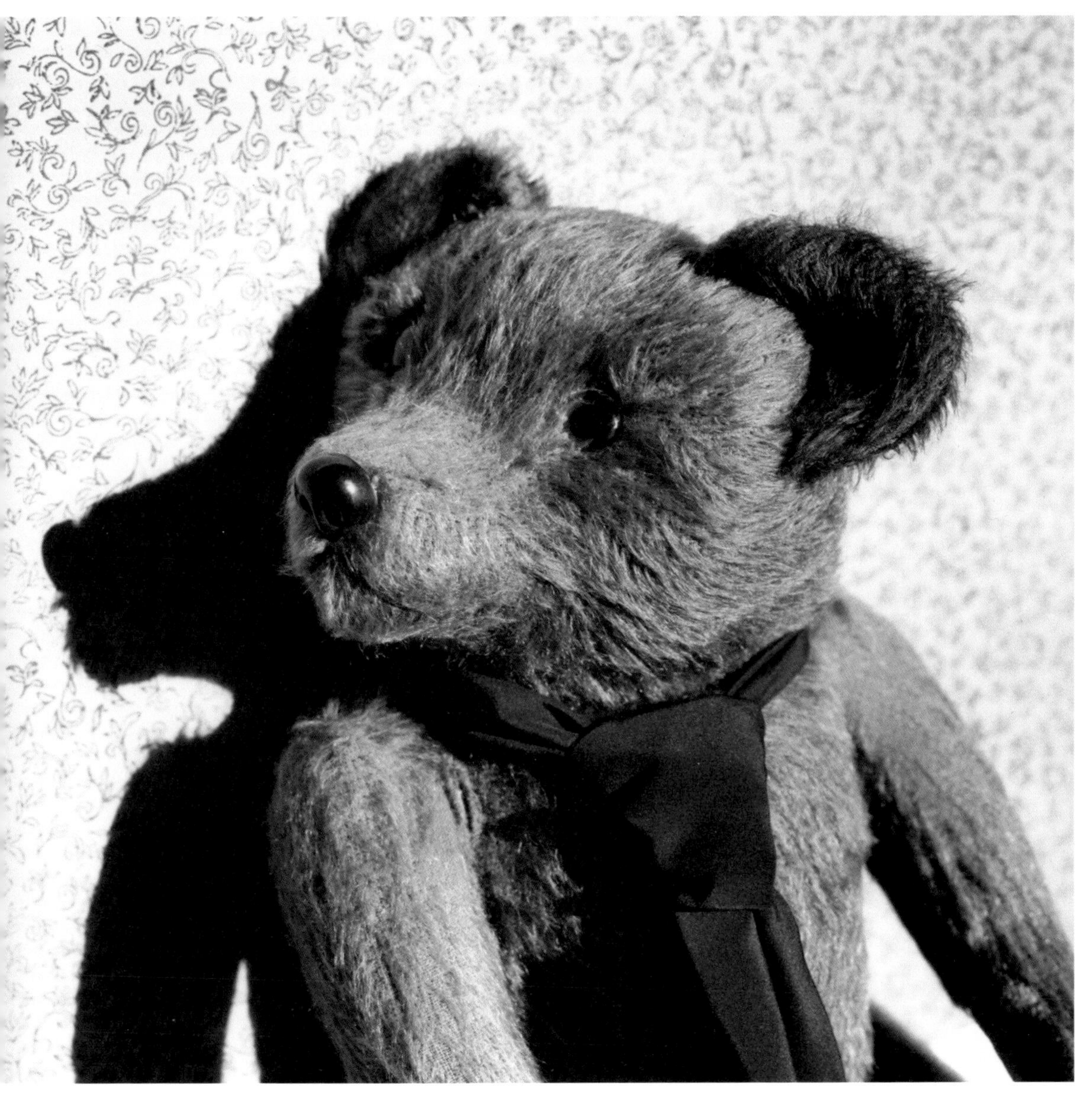

"You know, it doesn't do to stir memories

....

But perhaps my mother would be happy?

....

And she would tell us more

....

These bears, do you really believe we can give them a soul? "

Berthe, 2011

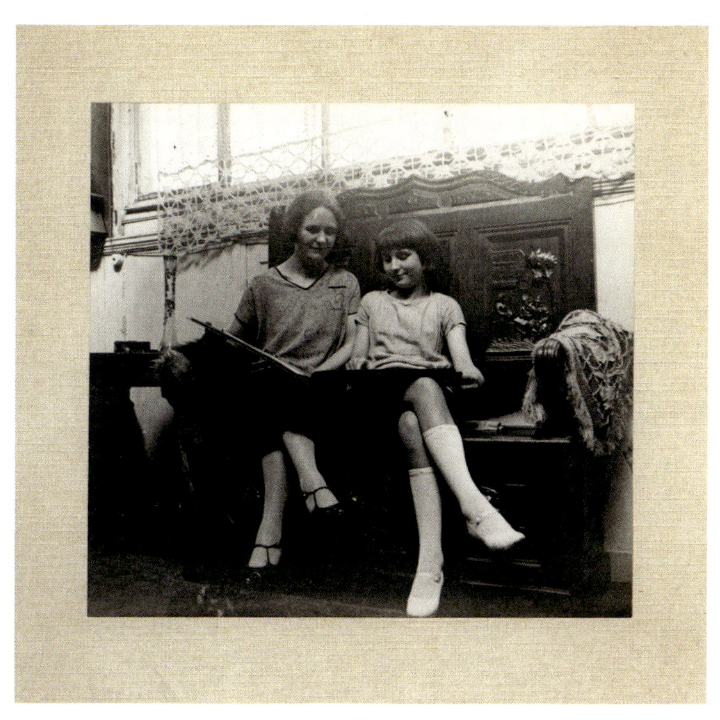

Berthe and her mother, 1926

The honourable old man
age: 96
belongs to:
Berthe

When I show Berthe a portrait
of her bear wearing a tie, she goes
to the closet and pulls out a
small plastic bag which holds
her first teddy bear, who had
been there for years.

"He takes the teddy bear out of the closet where he has been stored in tissue paper. He unwraps him and places him on his lap.

Left too long on a shelf in the bedroom closet, he is no more than a rag, moths have nibbled away his woollen snout, mice have gnawed at his paws and ears and pilfered stuffing from his belly.

The bear regains his former appearance, his slightly astounded look. But he reveals nothing to the person who has been with him and has protected him for so long … "

Sylvie Germain, *Magnus*, 2005

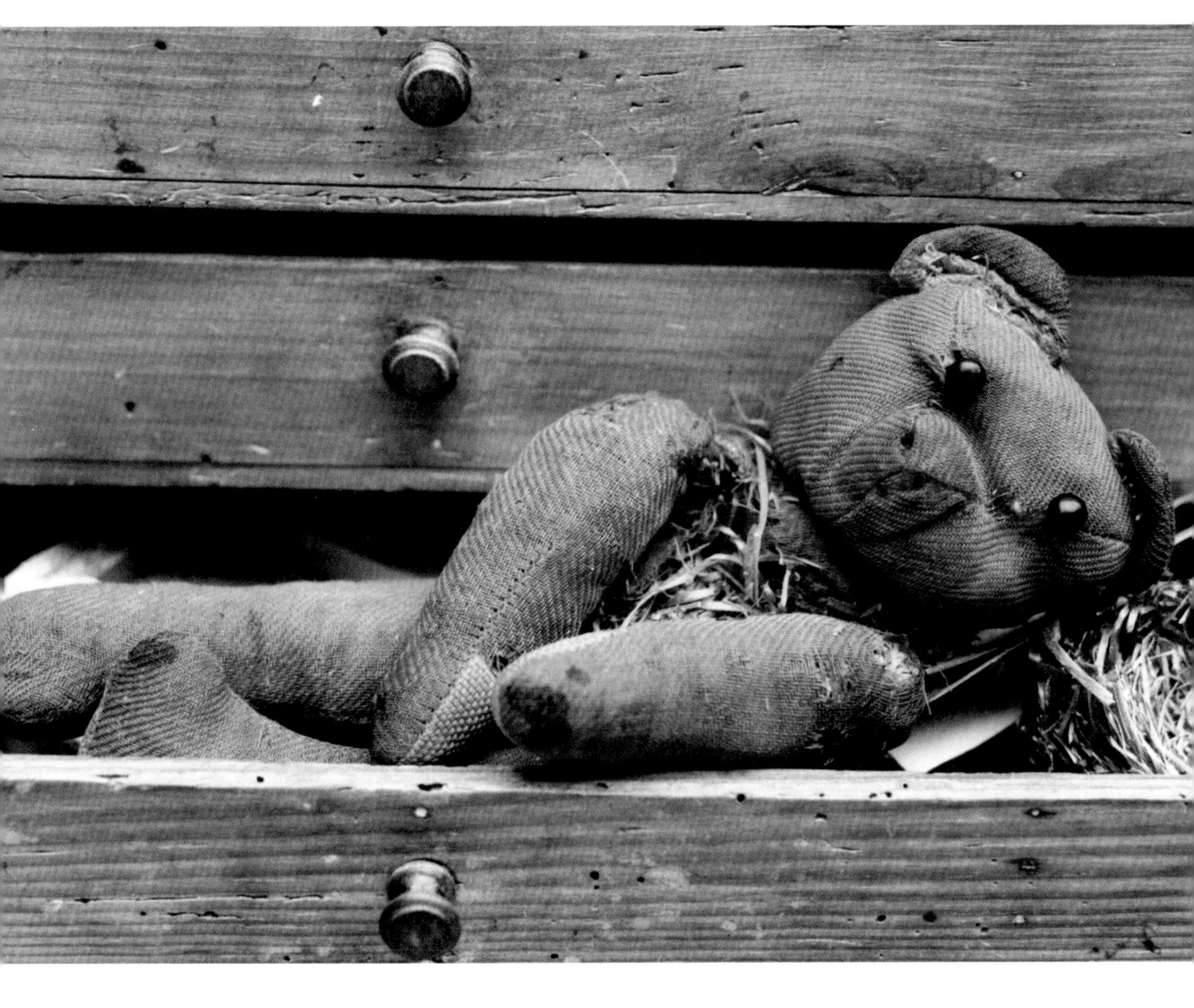

Jean-Jacques
age: 50
belongs to:
Hélène Benveniste

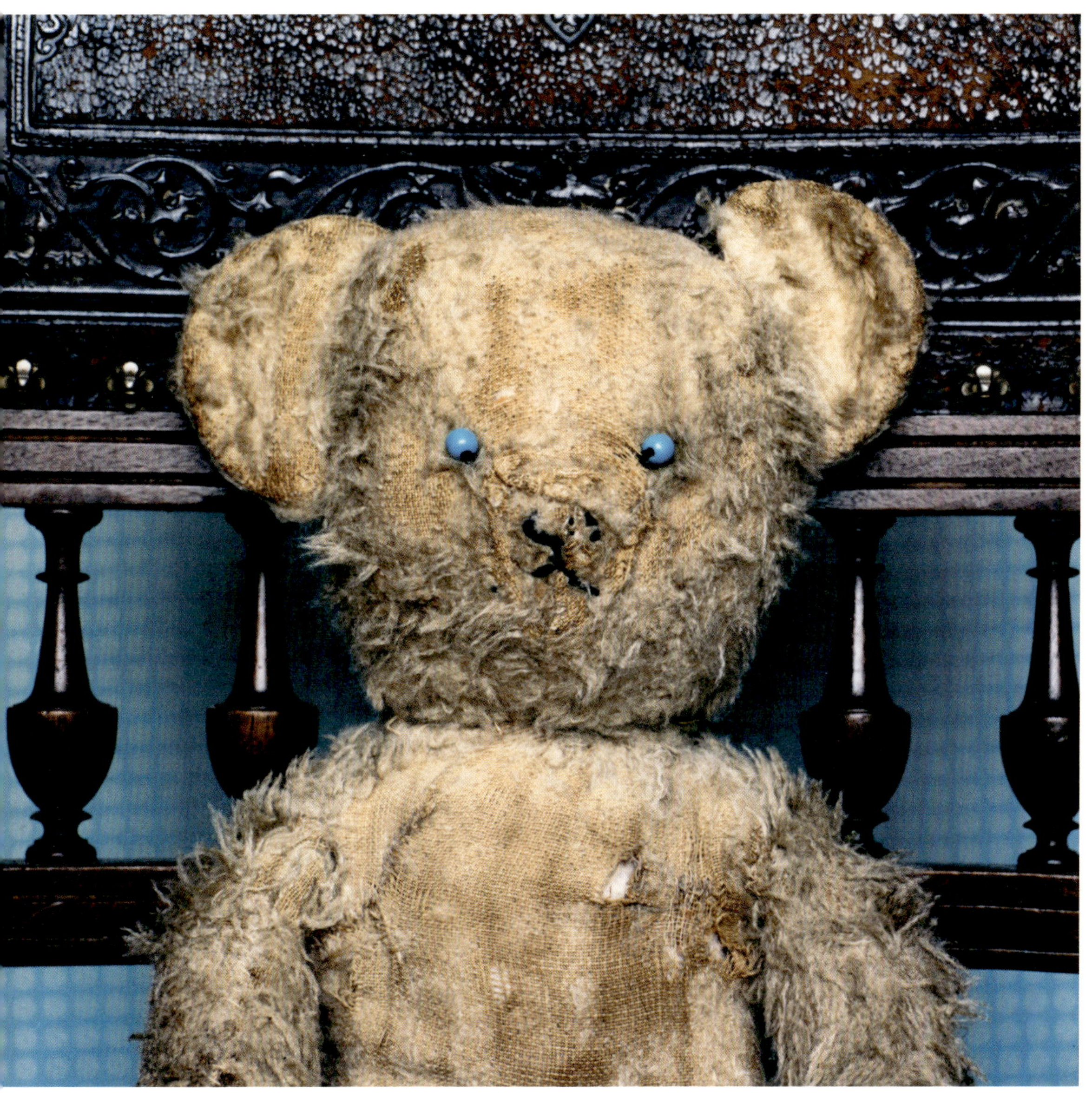

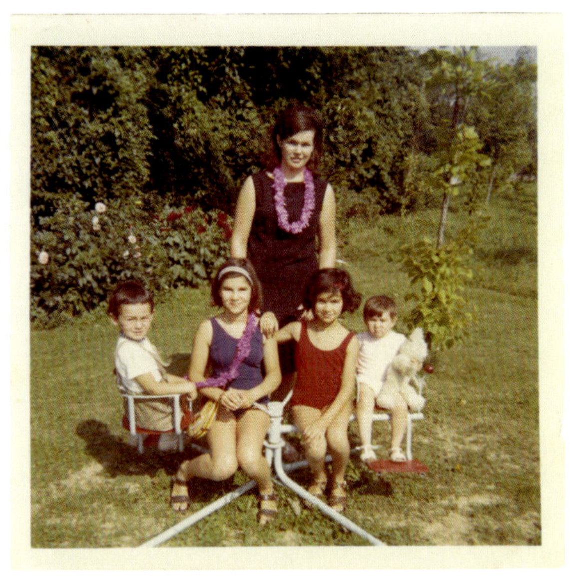

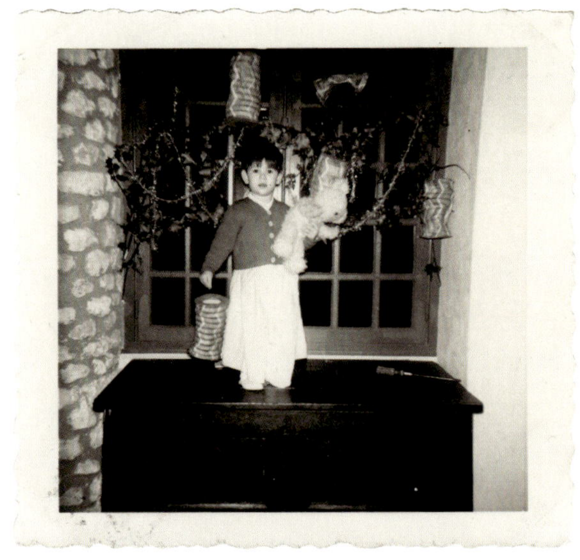

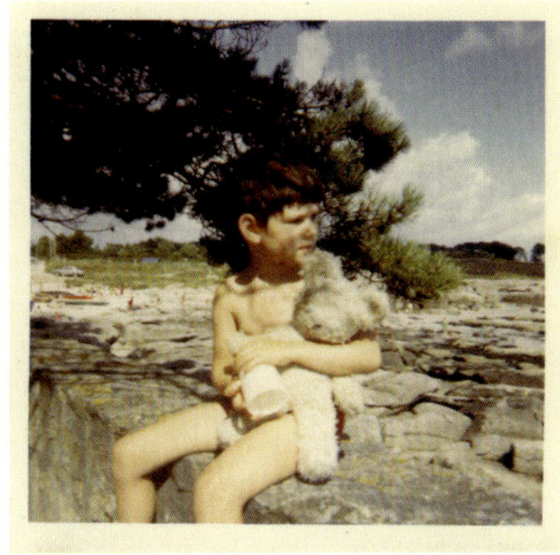

Jean-Jacques has known seas, mountains and countryside galore.
A tragic accident cost him his big blue eyes. After that I decided that
it would be better for him to stay at home.

Later, my first boyfriend found that he couldn't cope with three in a
bed. So there you have it – ten years in the cupboard! In 1989, a new
love arrived, who discovered the discreet presence of my bear. He was
brought back into the world.

Jean-Jacques says that having his photograph taken and it being
hung on the wall has been a 'validation of his inner self'. Generally,
people pay little attention to bears. Many friends stay in this house
and this is the first time that he has been made to feel that this is
also his home.

Hélène Benveniste

Belons + Agneau doux
age: 55
belongs to;
Hervé Guibert

"At first I used to sleep in my sister's bedroom. My earliest memories are of nightmares that woke me and made me fight with sleep. I sat on my bed waiting for the day to return. Agneaudoux was already with me: I was told that I got her for my first birthday. She is a small white lamb that had a flower on her pink nose, which I quickly pulled off. I used to dress her in my sister's dolls' clothes: thick sweaters and ski-pants for skiing, but also dresses, and swimwear because each year I took her to the seaside."

Hervé Guibert, *Mes parents*, 1996

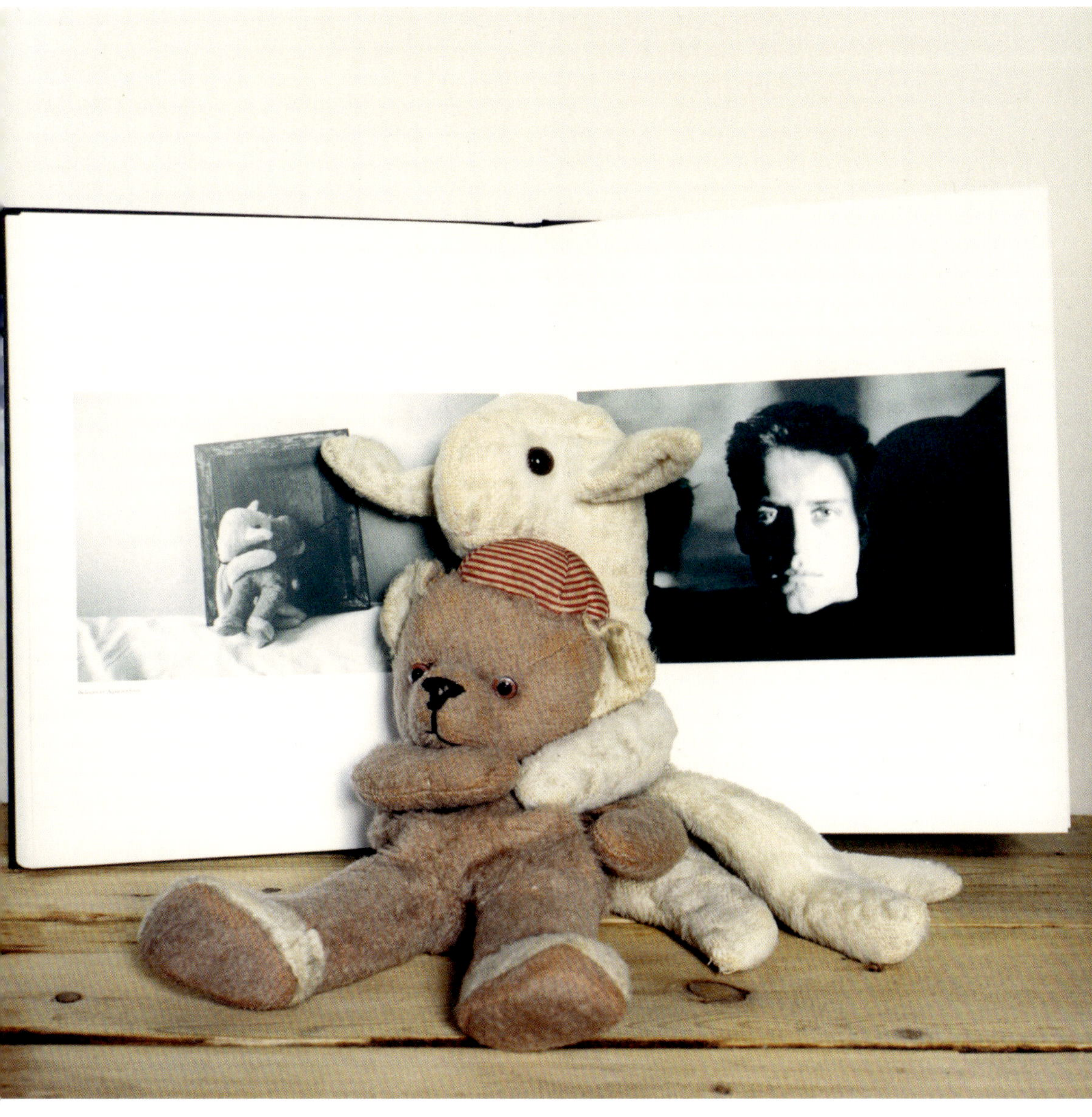

cf My parents, Gallimard
                                          1980

1st Cate   about Agrandons
(Christine   p. 23
Guibat
May)

Herri Guibert
'writer - photographer'
            1955 - 1991

of. 'L'image fantôme', le

(XR) 'LA PHOTO, INÉLUCTABLEM
              1999

. Suzanne & Louise, l

                    c un

July 10th
At Christine Guibut's place
+ gueudoux & the book
PHOTOGRAPHIES, Hervé Guibut
1993

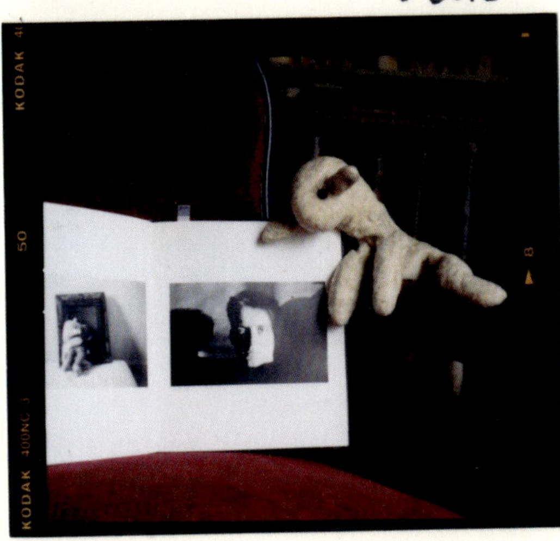

left: Belous + Agneudoux
@ Hervé Guibut
right: self portrait

The bear with the burned ear

age: 50

belongs to:

Eric Pendrizet

I remember it was in 1963, Eric's second Christmas. His father and I were newlyweds and had no money. So that he wouldn't find the bear, I had carefully hidden it in a cupboard behind a thick velvet curtain. In my excitement, I forgot to turn off the electric light. The inevitable happened, the bear's head was leaning against the lightbulb and its left ear began to scorch until the smell of burning attracted me to the bedroom. It was impossible to buy another one, we would have had to find a shop open on Christmas day! I found an old fur collar and made a cap to cover the blackened patch. To Eric, we said that a wounded bear with a gorgeous hat was the most precious of bears. And that's what he believed.

Chantal Perdrizet

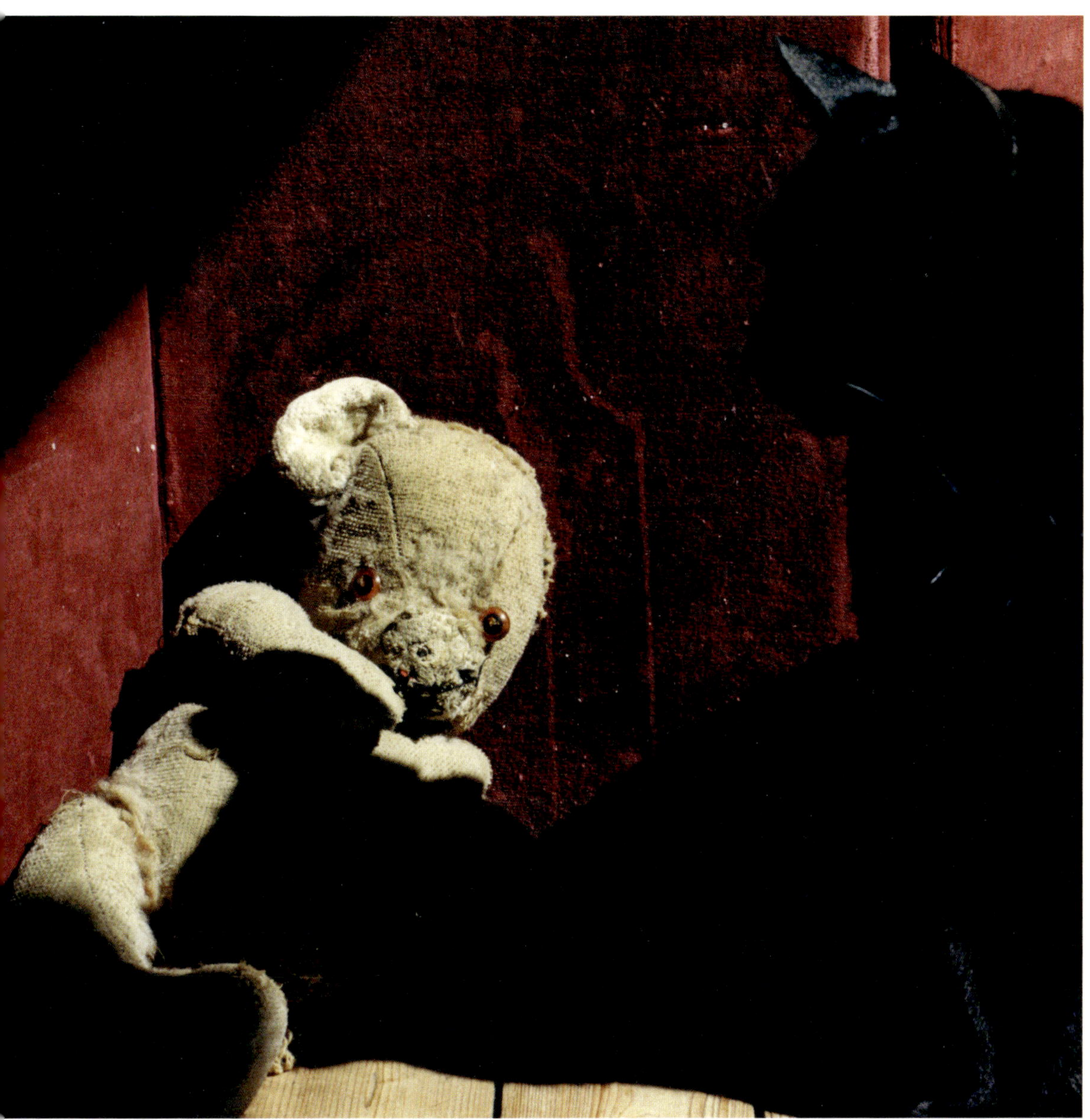

Martin
age: 57

belongs to:
Kitty

… the journeys with Martin in the back of the R4 – Baden-Baden, Luxembourg, the Black Forest, Saarbrücken, Paris, Switzerland, Limoges …

"with Martin, we're certain that the kids will be quiet"…

picnics with the bear …
the gingham dresses and white socks …
the visit to the doctor, x-rays with Martin in my arms …
the bailiffs: Martin neither seen nor known, hidden in the rubbish bags …
my lucky mascot, always the first to emerge after the storm …
the wear and tear of cuddles …

Memories with Martin, this is my life flashing by.

Kitty

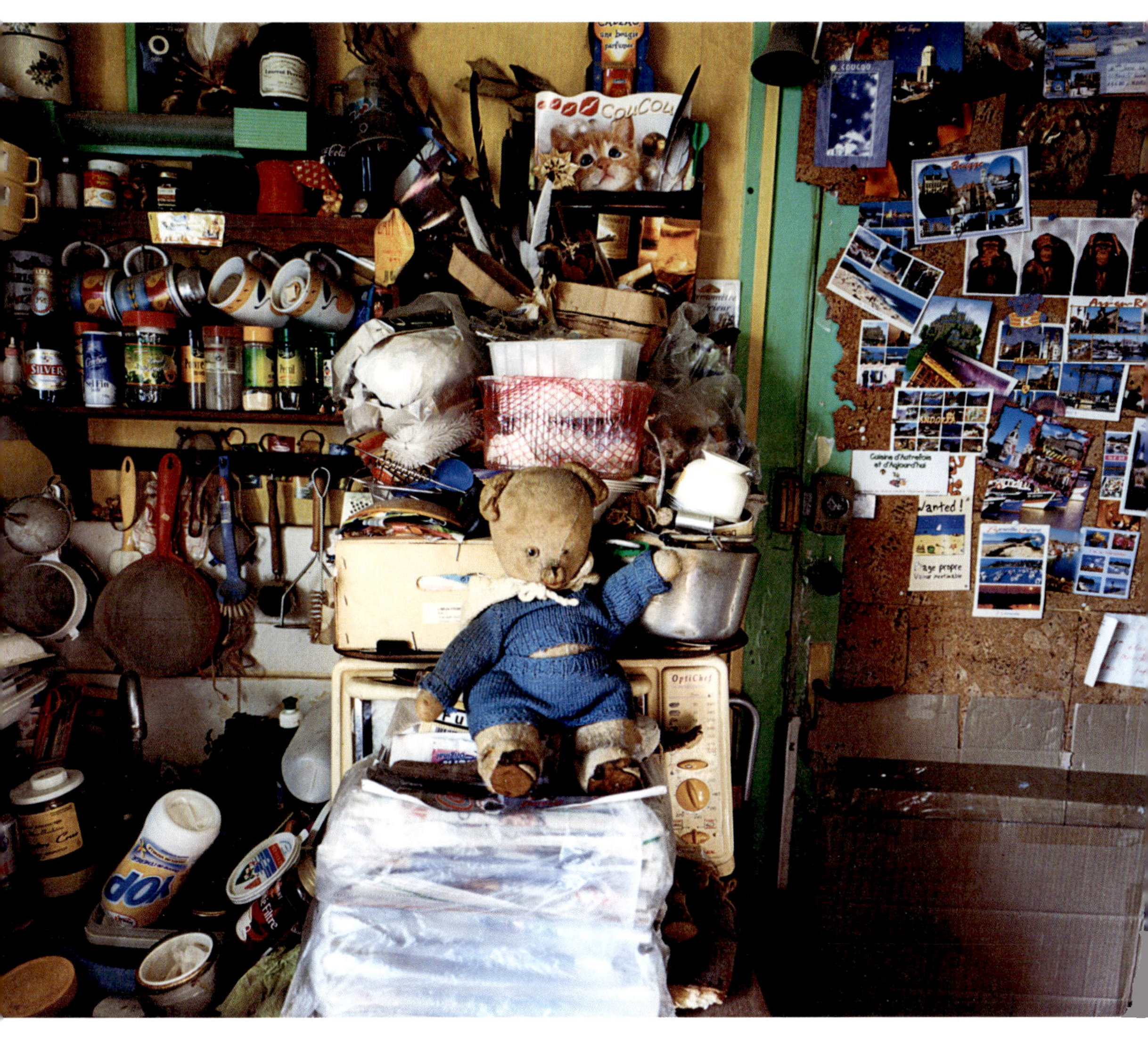

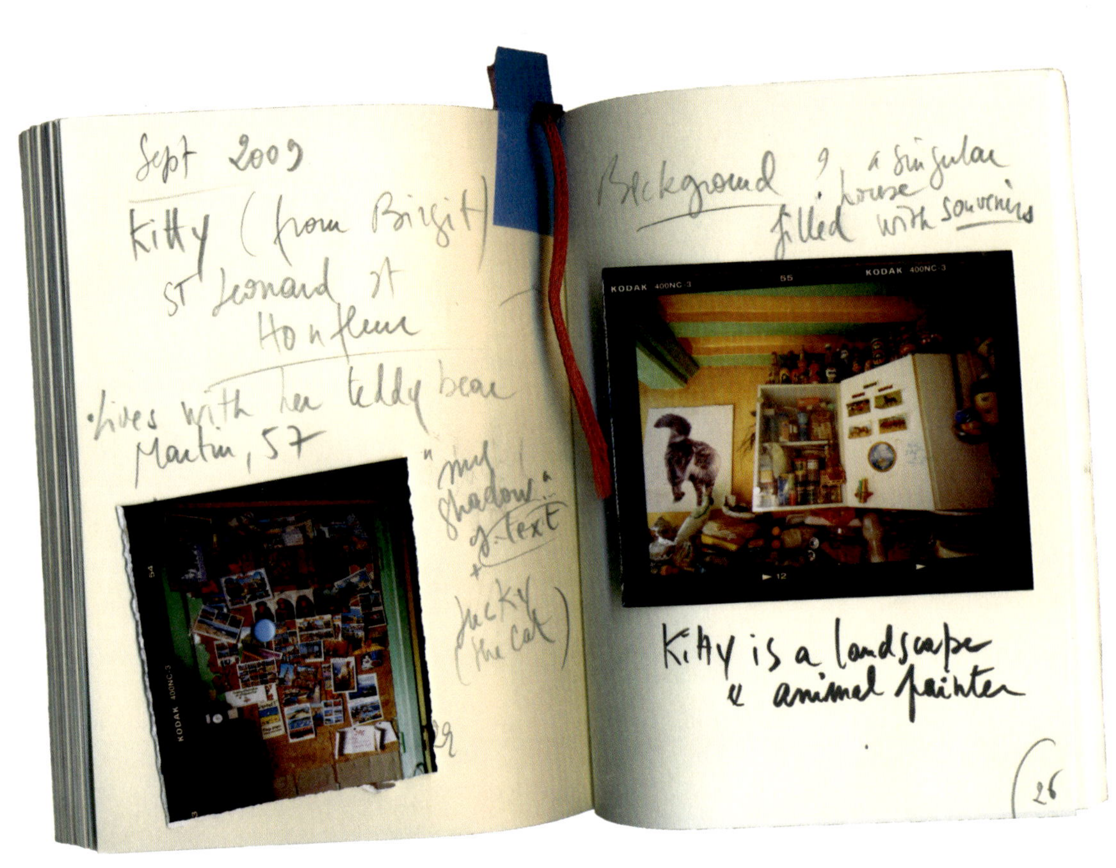

Sept 2009

Kitty (from Birgit)
St Leonard St
Honfleur

• lives with her teddy bear
Martin, 57

"my
shadow"
g. text
+

Jacky
(the cat)

Background ? a singular
house
filled with souvenirs

Kitty is a landscape
& animal painter

19-01-09

Martin, followed the thread of
my life.
I've always looked after him.
The only being I can count on
to tell everything about my life.
He is my shadow, my reflection.
The most loyal friend I've ever had.
— He is like a little brother to whom
one confides everything and who
promises not to repeat to the grown ups.
Above all he brings me luck.
He his my lucky pal —
For Sylvie / from Kitty

Dieter
age : 55
belongs to:
Jörg Hoyer

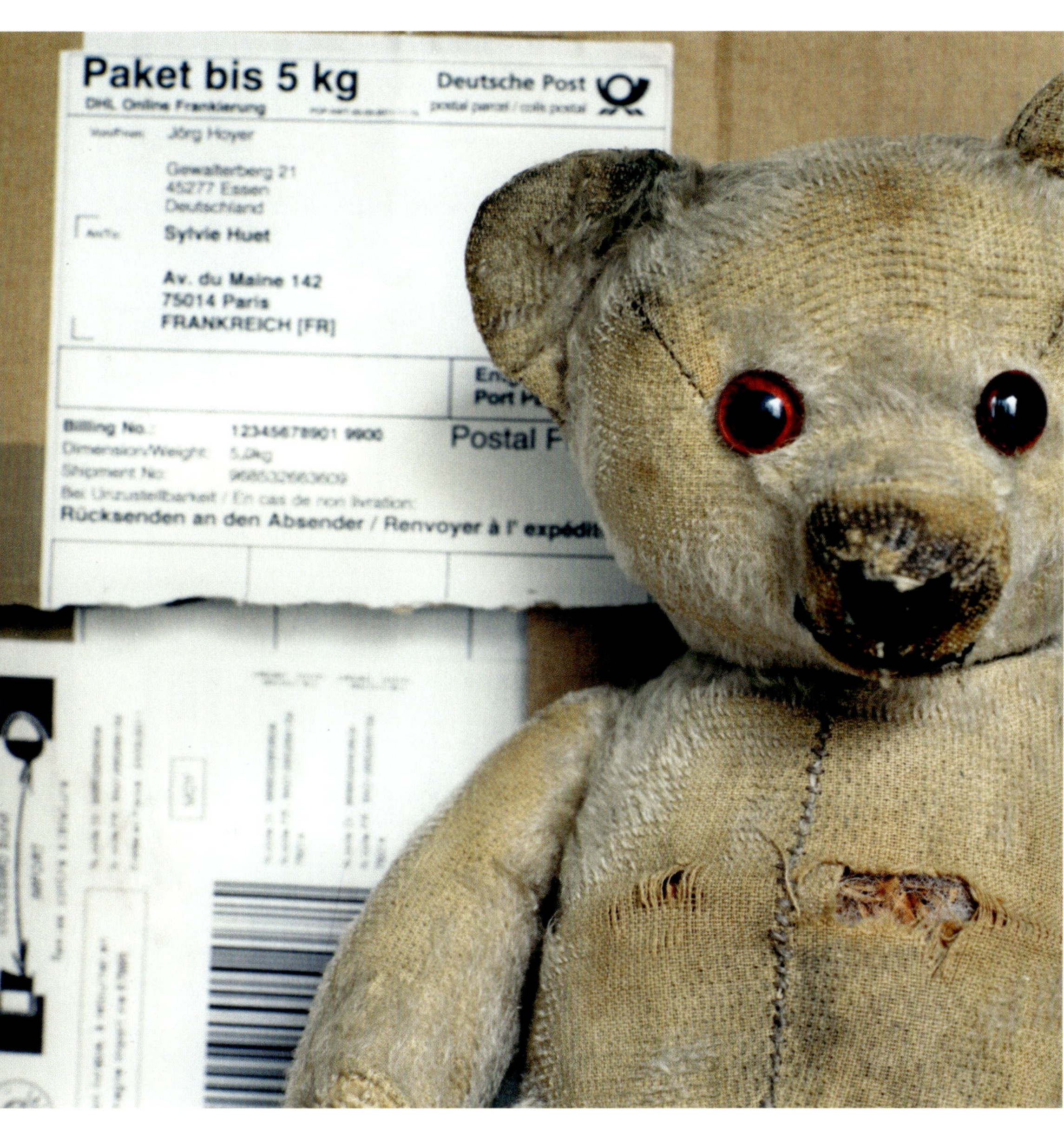

Paket bis 5 kg
DHL Online Frankierung
Deutsche Post
postal parcel / colis postal
Jörg Hoyer
Gewalterberg 21
45277 Essen
Deutschland
Sylvie Huet
Av. du Maine 142
75014 Paris
FRANKREICH [FR]
Postal F
Billing No.: 12345678901 9900
Dimension/Weight: 5,0kg
Shipment No:
Rücksenden an den Absender / Renvoyer à l' expédit.

From: sylvie huet <sy-huet@wanadoo.fr>
Date: 30 avril 2011 12:09:14
To: Jörg Hoyer
Subject: Dieter, a Teddy Bear – information for a french photographer

Hello,

I apologize for this quite weird e-mail but I'm in search of Jörg Hoyer who published in 2010 two photographs on the website : 'Young me Now me' where he also wrote about Dieter, his childhood teddy bear.

I'm not sure you are this person because I found several people bearing the same name in USA and Germany.

If by any chance you are... here is my request:

I am currently involved in a photobook project: childhood memory through portraits of worn, stitched, scarred teddy bears that grown-ups – 40-99 years old – have kept close at hand. I add an archive photograph showing the same teddy bear posing with the child. These old pictures give a resonance to the subject and bear witness to their truth.

I look forward to hearing from you.

So sorry if you don't like teddy bears!

Sylvie Huet

From: Jörg Hoyer
Date: 19 mai 2011 09:00:03
To: sylvie huet <sy-huet@wanadoo.fr>
Subject: Re: the Teddy Bear Project

Hi Sylvie,

What a surprise to hear from you just now! I find your project very interesting.

When I first saw the 'Young me Now me' blog the idea struck me to contribute with my Dieter photo. I had just completed scanning the photo collection from my cardboard box and my picture with Dieter came to mind. Being in my mid fifties, watching my 11 years old son made me look at my old pictures and wonder how life was for my parents and how my kids might feel for me now. When looking at these pictures some things catch my attention and I try to remember how those polyester trousers felt, how my toy train smelt and to see again the flute that my father played and that is now in my possession…

I like your bear photos! They make the bears look alive as they are in the imagination of a child. I am curious about what the picture of Dieter will be.

I live in Ruhrgebiet. I would love to see Paris some day. For now I will pay the postal ticket for Dieter. I am sure you will take good care of my old bear.

Take care!
Jörg

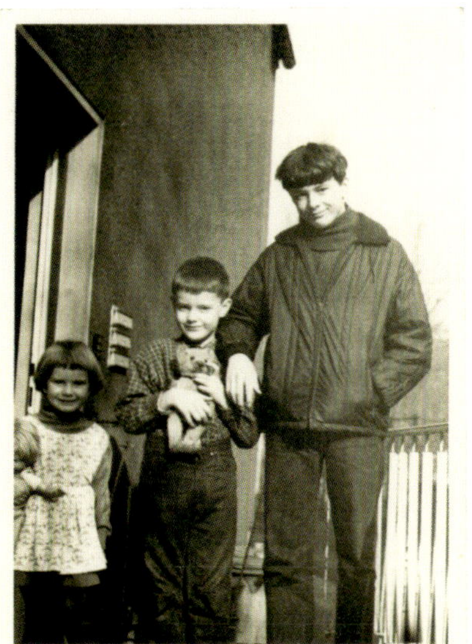
1960s, family picture with Dieter

2011/6/28 Sylvie Huet

Hi Jörg,

Dieter is in the box. He is supposed to arrive around next monday. It's a big responsibility for me. At the post office I was asked about 'the value of the object inside'. I said 'Invaluable!'

So please let me know when he is back?

Thanks !
Sylvie

2011/6/28 Jörg Hoyer

Thank you Sylvie, I appreciate your care for my old teddy and I am looking forward to getting him back. This is a nice experience. I told several of my friends how we met. Only some suspect you will trick me into something strange – most of them enjoy the idea and bring their childhood buddies to tell their story.

I hope Dieter has been helpful to develop the project a little further.
Jörg

"He must have been
mended by my mother
several times because he
was so worn out. Look at
the feet! As a teenager I
forgot him. Later I looked
inside the closets at my
parents' house to see
what I would find remind-
ing me of my youth.

I found Dieter wrapped
in a plastic bag. When
I saw him I shouted
"Dieter! Where have you
been !" It was such a joy
to see him again! I felt like a little boy. Since then Dieter stays with me
at home and is carefully looked after."

text published on www.zefrank.com/youngmenowme, 2010

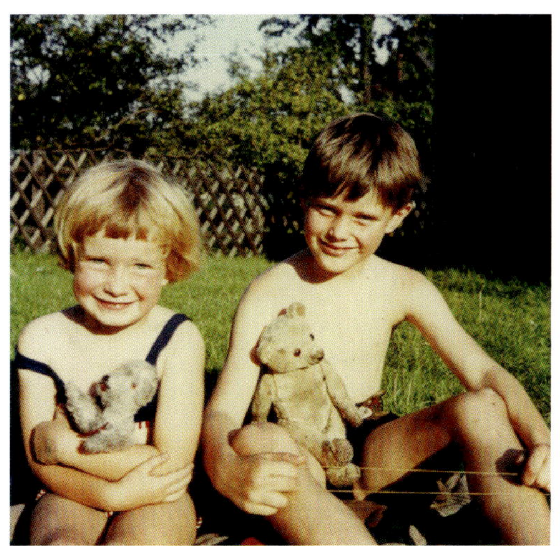

1961. Jörg and his sister
Kathrin with their new teddies

Gugus
age: 44
belongs to:
Rémi Coignet

One day, as I was scrolling
through Facebook, I came
across a teddy bear profile.
It was that of Rémi Coignet,
a photography critic. I knew
nothing about Rémi, other than
his writing, but contacted him
straight away to find out more.
The photograph was of GuGus,
Rémi's childhood bear who,
for a short while, found
himself in the limelight...

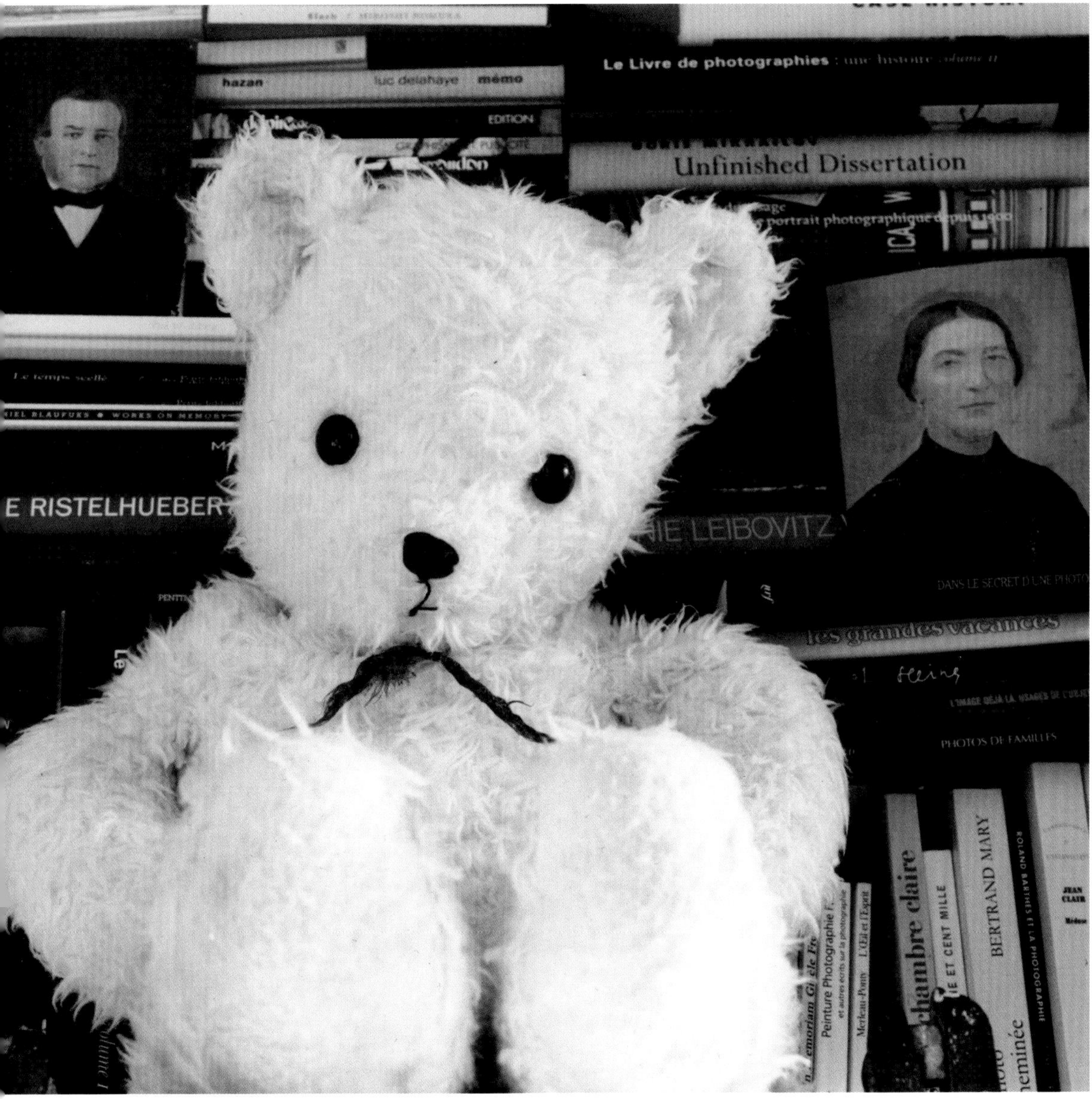
Le Livre de photographies : une histoire volume II
hazan
luc delahaye
mémo
EDITION
Unfinished Dissertation
Le temps scellé
WORKS ON MEMORY
E RISTELHUEBER
IE LEIBOVITZ
DANS LE SECRET D'UNE PHOTO
les grandes vacances
PHOTOS DE FAMILLES
Peinture Photographie
et autres écrits sur la photographie
Merleau-Ponty
L'Œil et l'Esprit
chambre claire
ET CENT MILLE
BERTRAND MARY
ROLAND BARTHES ET LA PHOTOGRAPHIE
JEAN CLAIR

Otto

age: unknown

belongs to:

Tomi Ungerer

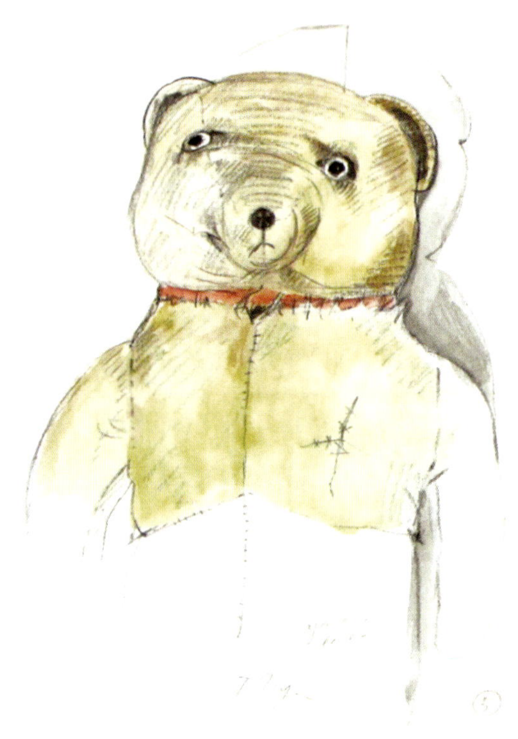

In Strasbourg, the world-renowned hero of the story *Otto* can be found. In the Tomi Ungerer Museum drawings of Otto can be seen everywhere. But who would suspect that the bear really exists?

Taken out of storage, he has been waiting for me since yesterday. Standing upright in his little house stuffed with tissue paper, he looks just like the drawings. But no! It is the drawings that look like him.

While I set up a pose for him, a group of children arrive on a school trip. Seeing the bear they shout: Otto! It's Otto! That's him! Madam, is that the real Otto!? They try to snap pictures on their mobiles to show that they've really seen him, but the attendant waves them away! I am the only one authorised to photograph him.

Otto emerges from his fictional world.

The teddy bear was found in a flea market in Canada by Tomi Ungerer, between 1975 et 1976. Because it ressembled his childhood bear, he bought it and used it as a model for his character Otto. Since the 1990s, it has been preserved by the Strasbourg museum in the Tomi Ungerer collection of toys.

Thérèse Willer

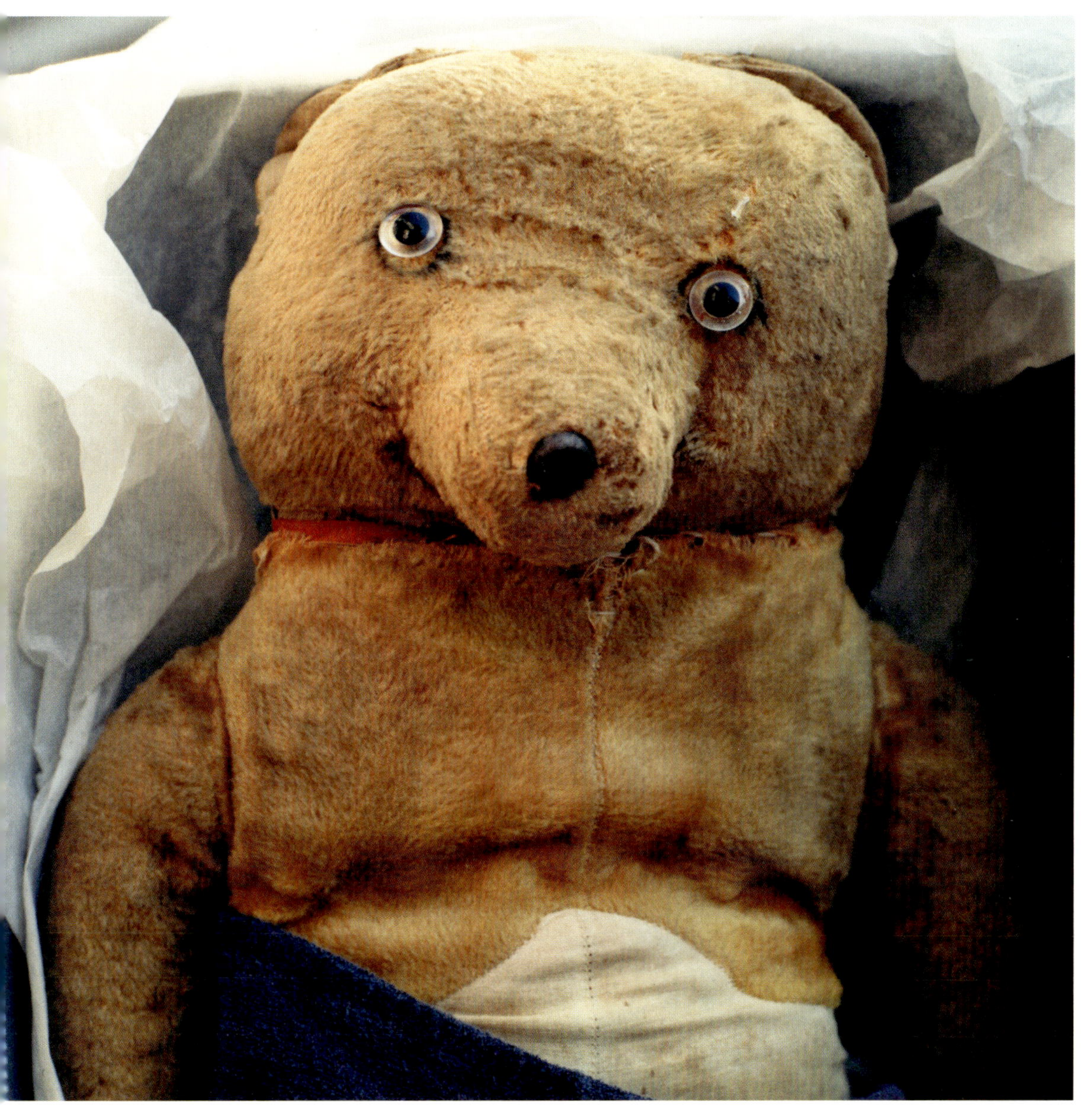

Teddy

age: 75

belongs to:

Mylène Demongeot

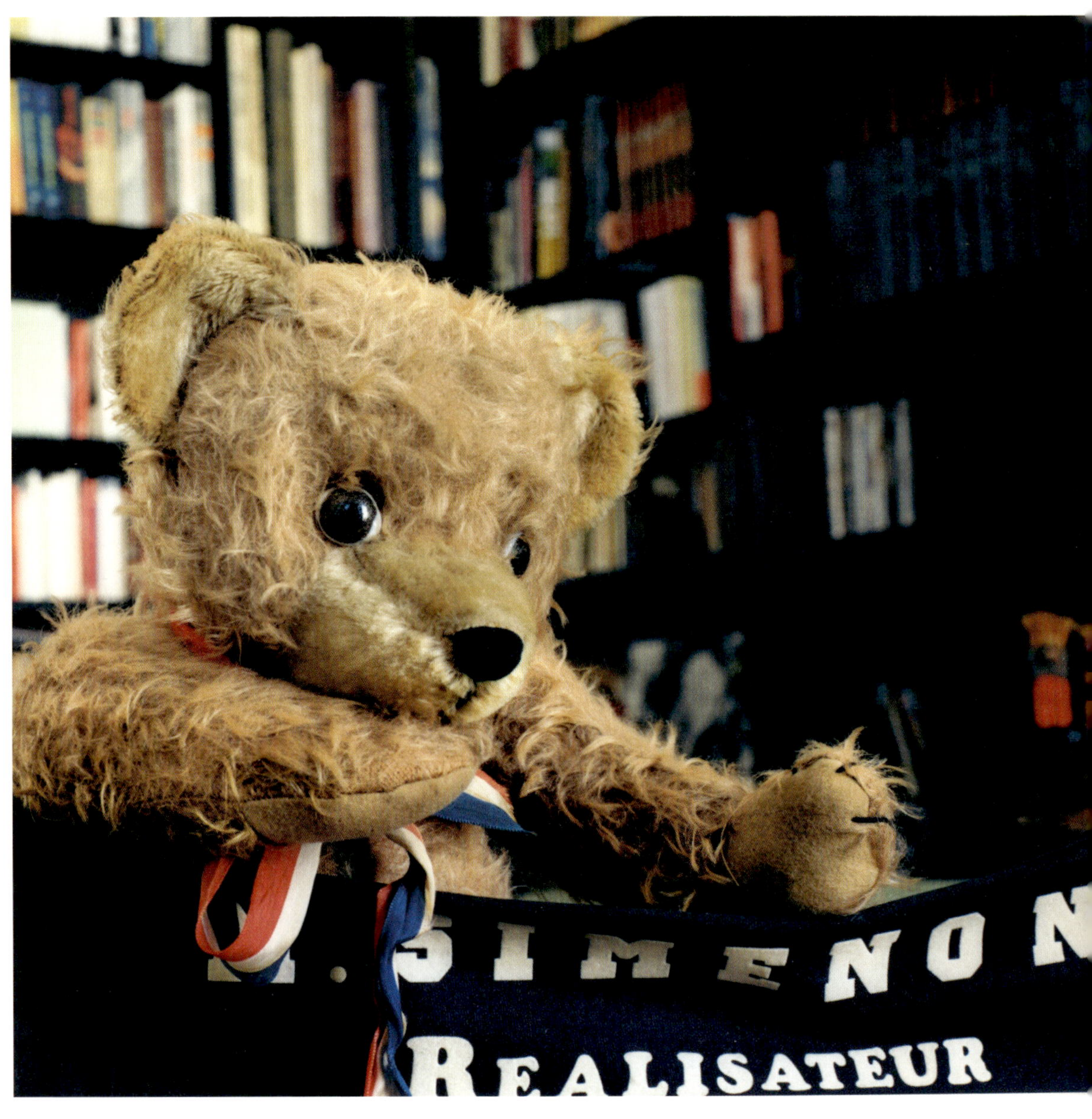
N. SIMENON
REALISATEUR

Paris, June 2011

Dear Mylène

From reading all your interviews, I know how attached you are to your child-hood teddy, to the point that you even want to be buried with him. (...) There will be some famous 'friends' in my forthcoming book... but, in truth, I'm not looking for stars, simply for stories about bears.

I would be delighted to meet your childhood friend and see him join with my funny little family. Here are some portraits. I hope they will appeal to you and Teddy.

Sylvie Huet

....

Dear Sylvie,

All right. My teddy can be photographed by you! He was a little 'refreshed' by a specialist and has pride of place in my living room. I would love to show you!

I seem to remember that Teddy was given to me by my grandmother when my father picked me up from Nice to take me to Paris ... so I was four. And I saw my dear Nonna on her deathbed in 1944.

This is my Teddy, a sacred object. He will travel with me to the end of my life.

In friendship

Mylène

Nana
age: 60
belong to:
Jean Paul Gaultier

Nana is a star, I knew it. I will have to
travel to him if I want him in the book.
New York? Madrid? Stockholm?
...
Jean Paul agreed! I chose Stockholm.

At Arkitektur- Och Design Center, in the
protective glass case of the 'boudoir',
the little transvestite bear can be admired
by thousands of fans. Does the public
know that?:
"Without Nana, this adventure of
Conical falsies would not have existed."

To photograph him up close. I chose
the day the exhibition is being taken down.

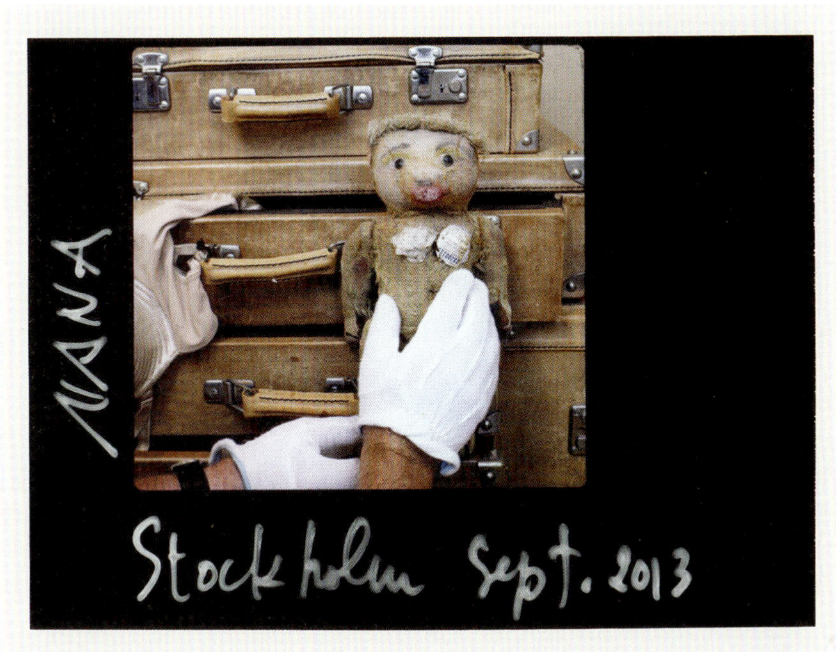

"I will put your project to Jean Paul. Note that if he accepts, Nana has been on tour with 'The Fashion World' since 2011 and will be until 2015."
Jelka Music, PR director at Jean Paul Gaultier, Paris 2012

"Jean Paul Gaultier's instructions are very strict: only one person is allowed to touch Nana ... This is in some way the most important piece in the collection."
Thierry-Maxime Loriot, the exhibition curator, Stockholm 2013

"My Teddy? I still have him, he is called Nana. He was my first model! First, he was submitted to all the assaults of cosmetics. I used to try my grandmother's *Rouge Baiser* on him. I used to borrow her face powder … I implanted bits of string on his head, as if he had hair, after having dyed them. I carried out my first attempts as a stylist on him. I put some prostheses on him: I made him some false pointed breasts, Madonna-style. Later, I always drew breast-shells like that. I cut out a small circle from a newspaper, I put some foam inside. And I stapled the whole thing onto my bear."

Did that please your parents?

It was ok … On the other hand they would not have wanted me to do that on a doll. It is a transvestite bear anyway!

Jean Paul Gaultier

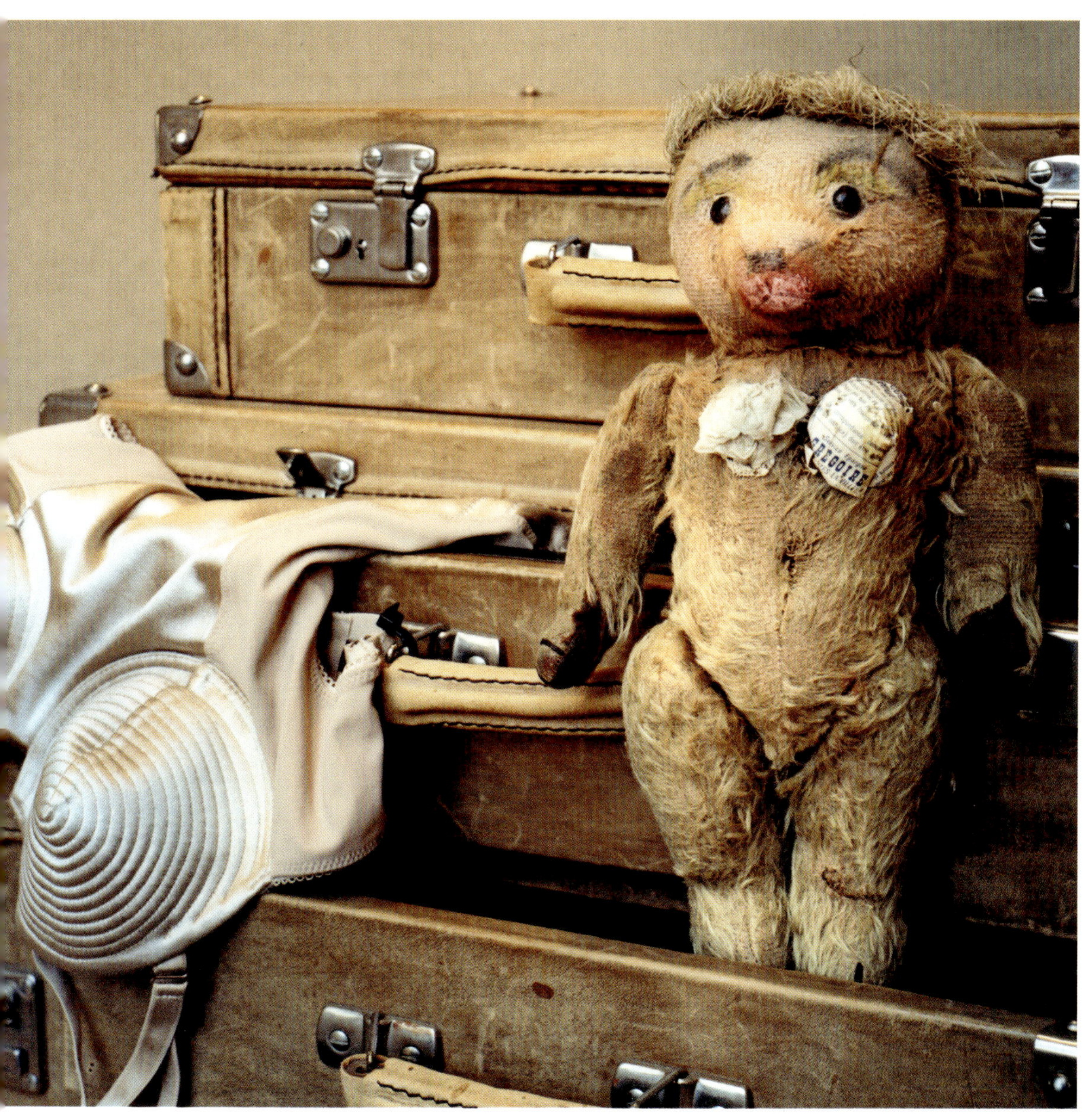

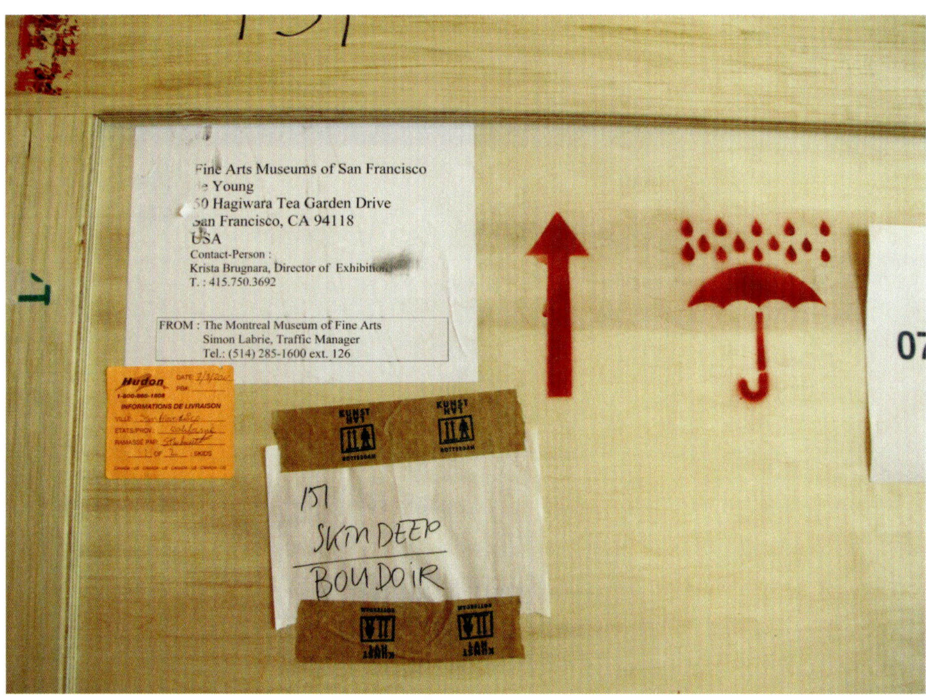
Fine Arts Museums of San Francisco
de Young
50 Hagiwara Tea Garden Drive
San Francisco, CA 94118
USA
Contact-Person :
Krista Brugnara, Director of Exhibition
T. : 415.750.3692
FROM : The Montreal Museum of Fine Arts
Simon Labrie, Traffic Manager
Tel.: (514) 285-1600 ext. 126
Hudon
1-800-868-1808
INFORMATIONS DE LIVRAISON
151
SKIN DEEP
BOUDOIR

Nana,

As I fly out of Stockholm
you are already on your way
to New York. If you had not
helped create your dad
the ENFANT TERRIBLE DE LA MODE,
your life would have been
less glamourous. Well done!
I'm happy to see you join
this band of dears,
all stars to someone
and for a life time.

S

The bear
age: 98
belongs to:
Noëlle Bittner

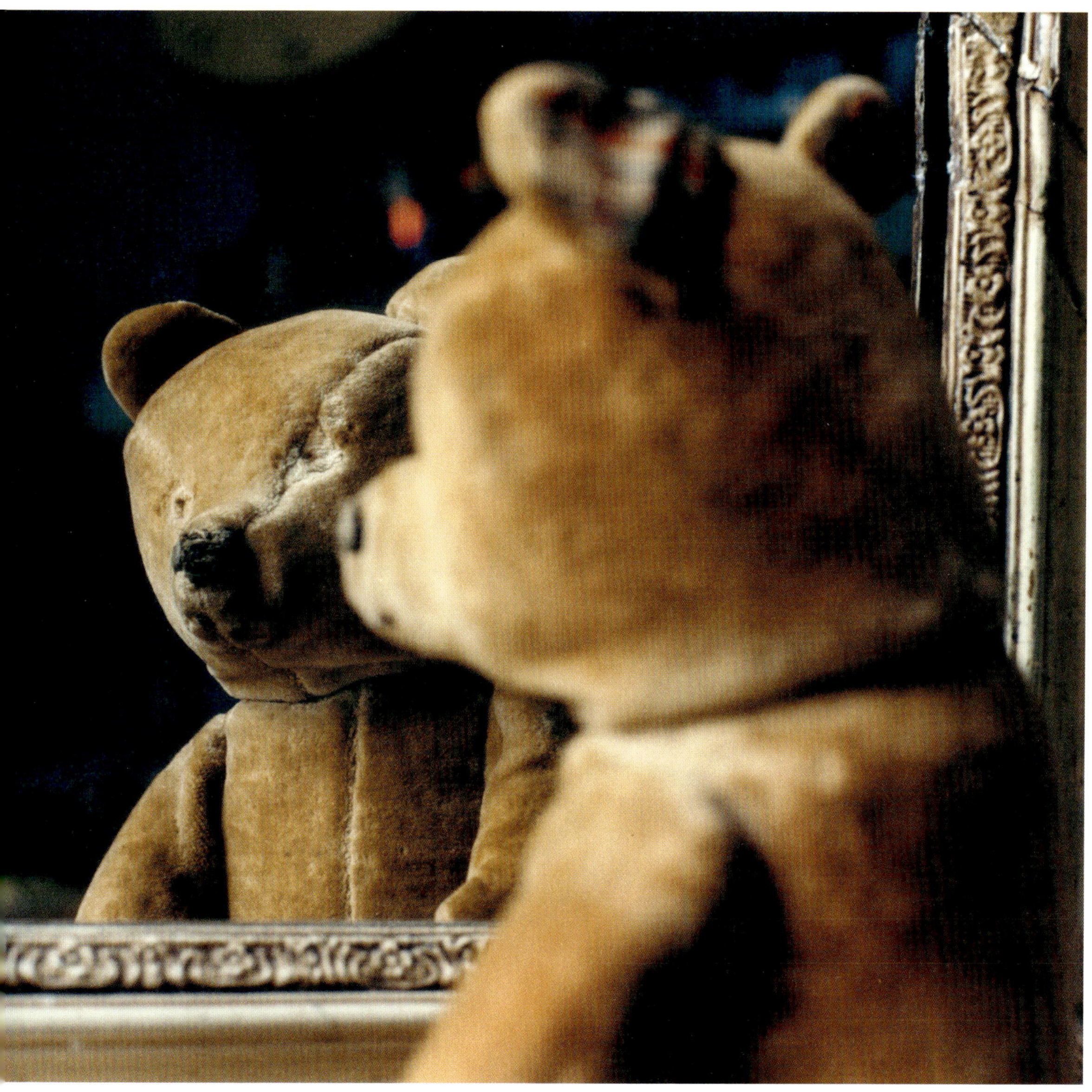

He is still called 'The bear'. He belonged to my older sister and before that to my mother, who is now 98 years old. That means that he would be Russian, from before the Revolution. It doesn't seem as if he came from a factory, with his straw, I rather imagine that he came from the hands of a very talented housekeeper.

Although I was a little more interested in cars than girls' dolls, he meant a lot to me. My mother made little fuss over him, but I cared for my little bear. Some time in his life, he lost an ear.

My mother had the ingenious idea to split the remaining ear and line each half with a Scottish tartan. This is the only bear I know with Scottish ears. I was 17 when I 'loaned' him to a little boy who had just lost his mother. When I got him back, several years later, he had suffered, all smeared with felt pen, and he'd lost his glass eyes. I cleaned him as best as I could and though I searched in flea markets, I never could find eyes for him, so I gave up. I don't mind, when he looks at me, he hasn't changed at all.

Noëlle Bittner

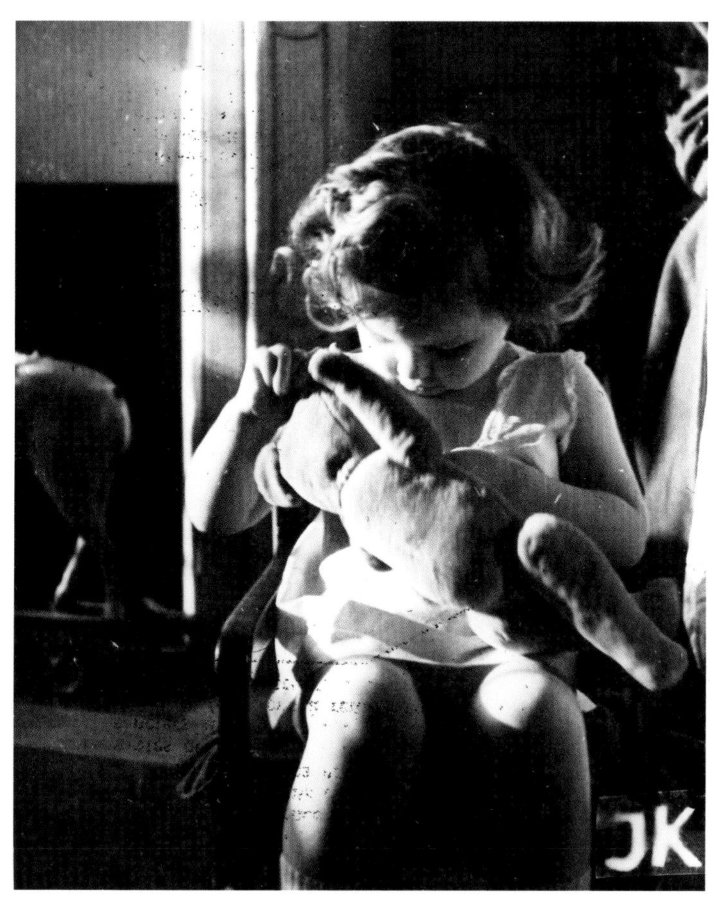

Brigitte, Noëlle's sister
and 'The bear', 1960

Tigger
age: 60
belongs to:
Jennie Maizener

Jennifer was about to leave the room when she heard me telling my story. She mentioned the cellar where her 'Tigger' would almost certainly be found. Her off-hand manner could have put me off. Then, right out of the blue, she added, "It is a story of guilt." This intrigued me.

Within minutes Jennie had travelled through the veils of time to relive a forgotten episode from her childhood. She didn't stop then until she had unearthed the tiger from amongst the thirty or so boxes piled up in the cellar. Once again he had his place on the geometrically-patterned bedspread which had welcomed him in the past.

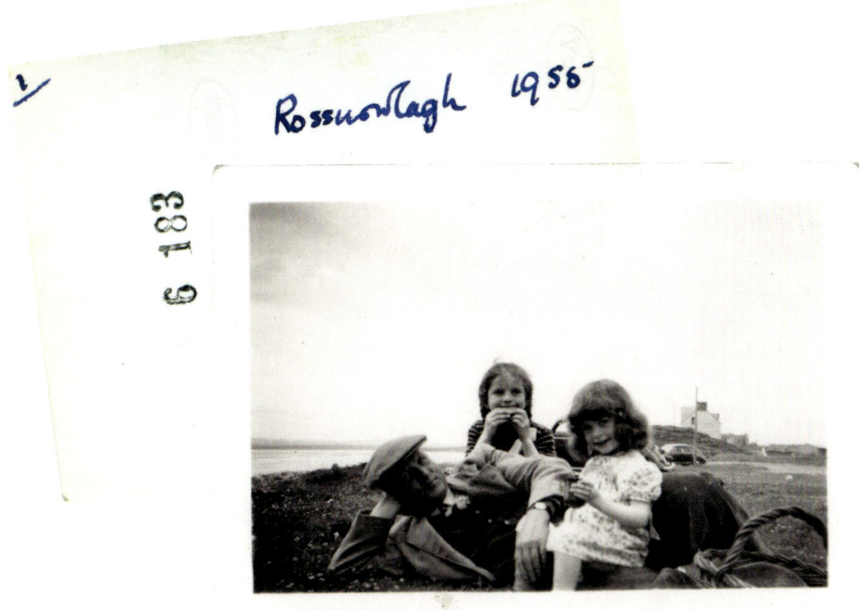

Rossnowlagh 1955
6 183

We went into Worcester shopping for Christmas

In the window of this big old toyshop ~~just near~~ in Worcester ~~A.D. Jones~~, there was a huge panda. It took up the whole window, with a background of cotton wool snow & glitter ~~& it seemed to & hold out its arms~~. So when my mother asked what I wanted for Christmas I didn't hesitate. — The panda. Oh, yes dear, she said vaguely. My sister managed to get a peek at Mum's Christmas list & there it was Jennie: cuddly toy. I hardly slept on Christmas Eve, constantly moving my toes down to the bottom of the bed to see if "Father Christmas" had delivered what I hankered for. At least I felt a weight on my feet & ~~moved stealthily down the bed to feel the lumpy parcel & the bulging stocking~~ but the light filtered through the curtains I saw not white with black patches, but orange with black stripes. My mother had made me a Tiger. After a quarter of an hour of snuffling desolation I looked at it carefully. It had appealing green almond shaped eyes. Mum ~~must have~~ spent hours making it. She thought I was going to be delighted. So I pretended to be really pleased. It sounded hollow & unconvincing to me, but she didn't seem to notice. Poor Tigron. I think after I loved him all the more, for not having loved him at first. *Jennie*

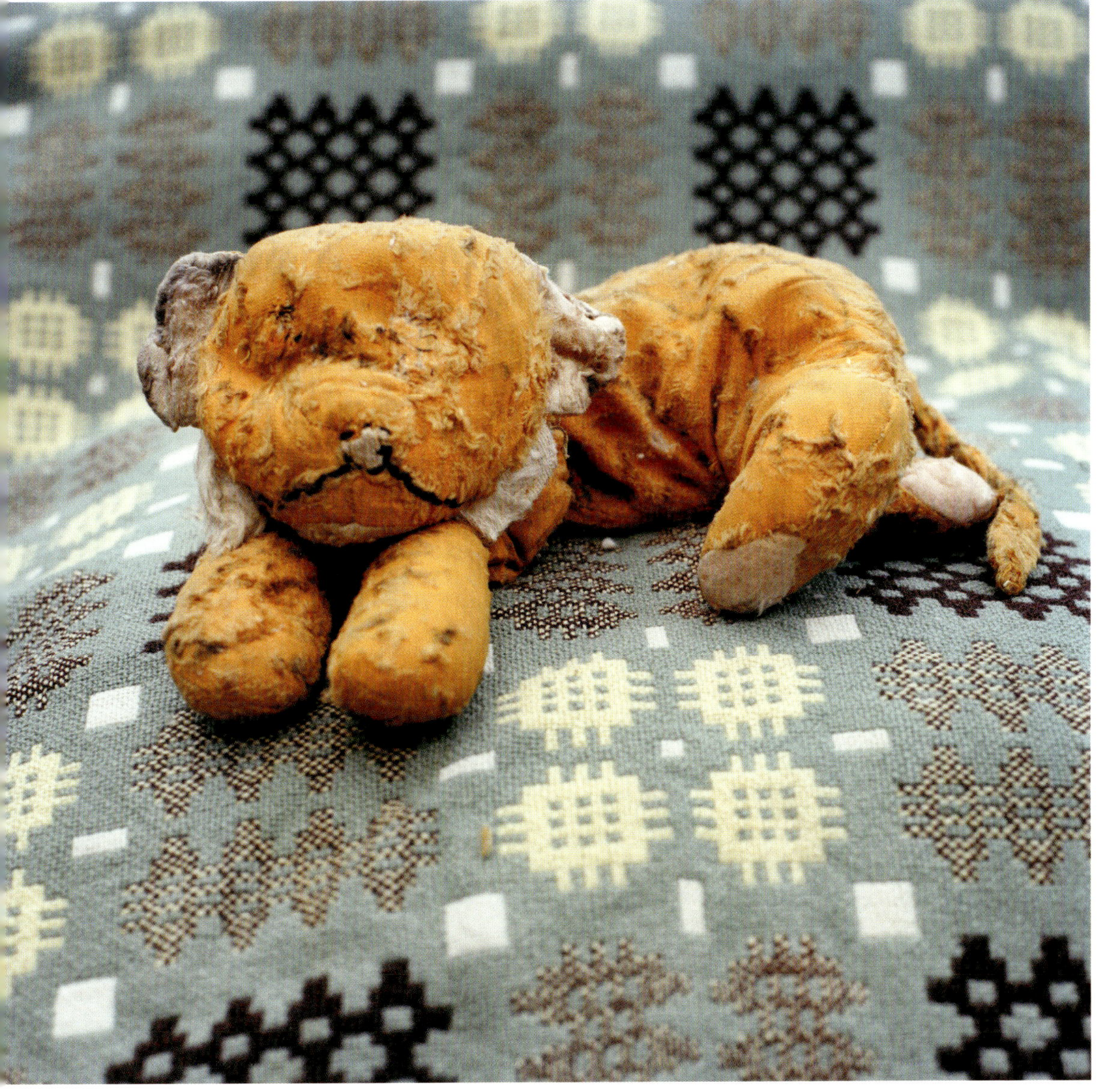

The faithful friend

age: 58

belongs to:

Jean-Marie Libout

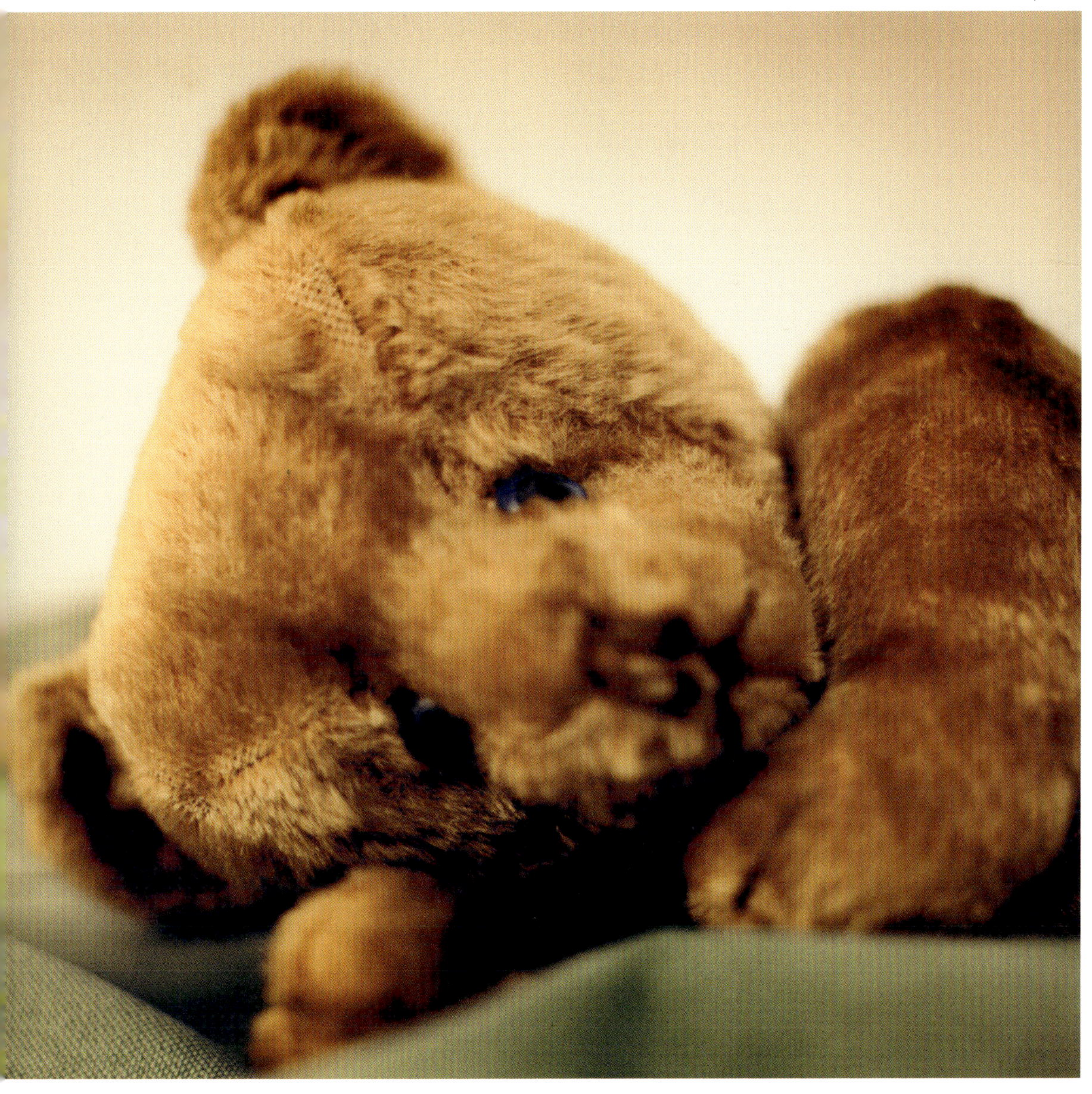

From: Jean-Marie Jibou
Date: 21 avril 2010 08:43:14
To: sy-huet@wanadoo.fr
Subject: About my teddy

Hello,

What can I say about this bear who has followed me everywhere? On holidays, when I was a child, he would travel in a metal trunk and I would be reunited with him on the banks of Lake Geneva. And the poor thing would be subjected to innumerable operations with me as the anaesthetist and my father as the surgeon.

At each moment of my life, from the most beautiful to the most foolish, he has always been there on that same shelf.

But I prefer to express myself in rhyme.

Jean-Marie Jibou

Just like that, now it's you who is the star!
You pose, I've no idea where, in front of the photographer!
They will talk about you, maybe a little bit about me,
But will you know how to tell them about our moments of madness!

You seem unaware that your success
Is only due to ma patience, always taking you with me.
And at times when life gets hard
To sleep in the wind, to go to bed in the streets?

If you've never had a nickname or surname
It's because you are you, my faithful friend
All that is in me, nameless memories,
So no need for me to give you a name.

Jean-Marie.

Jubilee

age: 78

belongs to:

Jane Goodall

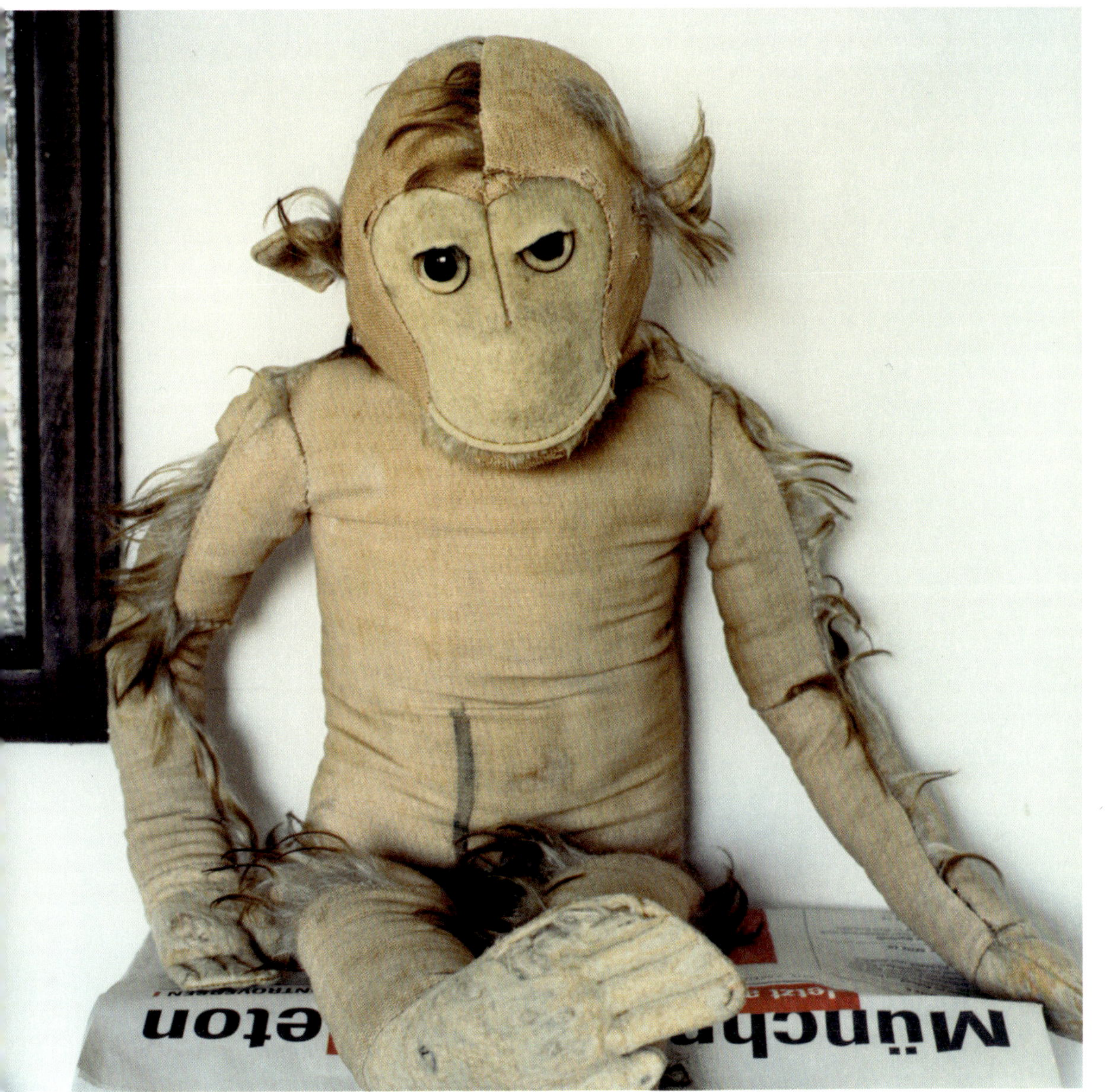

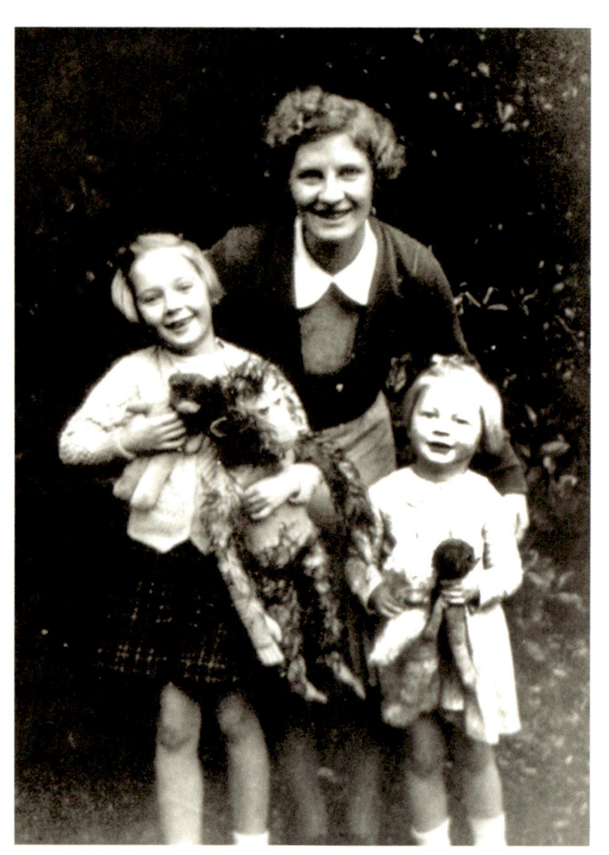

Jubilee, 6 yrs
Bournemouth?

My father gave me Jubilee
in 1935 when I was 18 months
old.   I loved him from the
start.   I carried him
everywhere. Today he is
bald from so much loving -
and perhaps a little
moth damage! He sits on
a chair in my room in
Bournemouth, UK - where I
grew up.

Jane Goodall

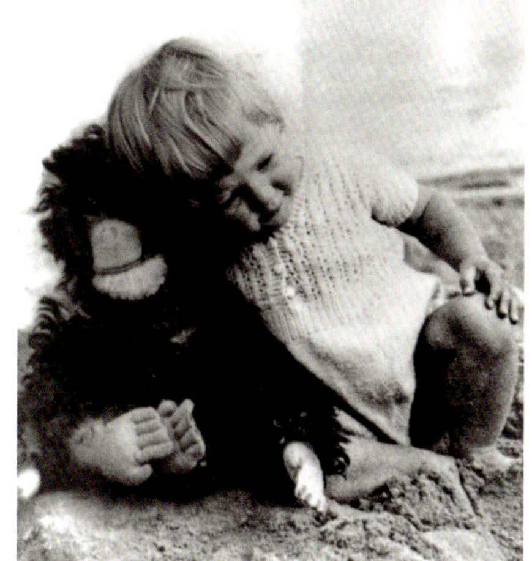

How Jubilee came to Munich

Jubilee first became world-famous thanks to his supporting role in
Munich-based director Lorenz Knauer's documentary *Jane's Journey*.
The idea came up to preserve Jubilee as he was, with all the damage
and wrinkles he had acquired in the course of his long life, but at
the same time trying to prevent his health and looks from further
deterioration, especially his foot, which suffers from an injury caused
by a bird that attacked him in his youth.

The best possible address for this kind of careful treatment is Barbara
Wahnemühl's 'Teddy-Clinic' in Duisburg, Germany. It was here that
'Mr. H', Jane Goodall's famous mascot ventured.

Monica Lieschke, 2013

Munich
December 2013
Posing for Sophie before my gay at the Teddy clinic Jubilee

Prosper

age: 77

belongs to:
Véronique

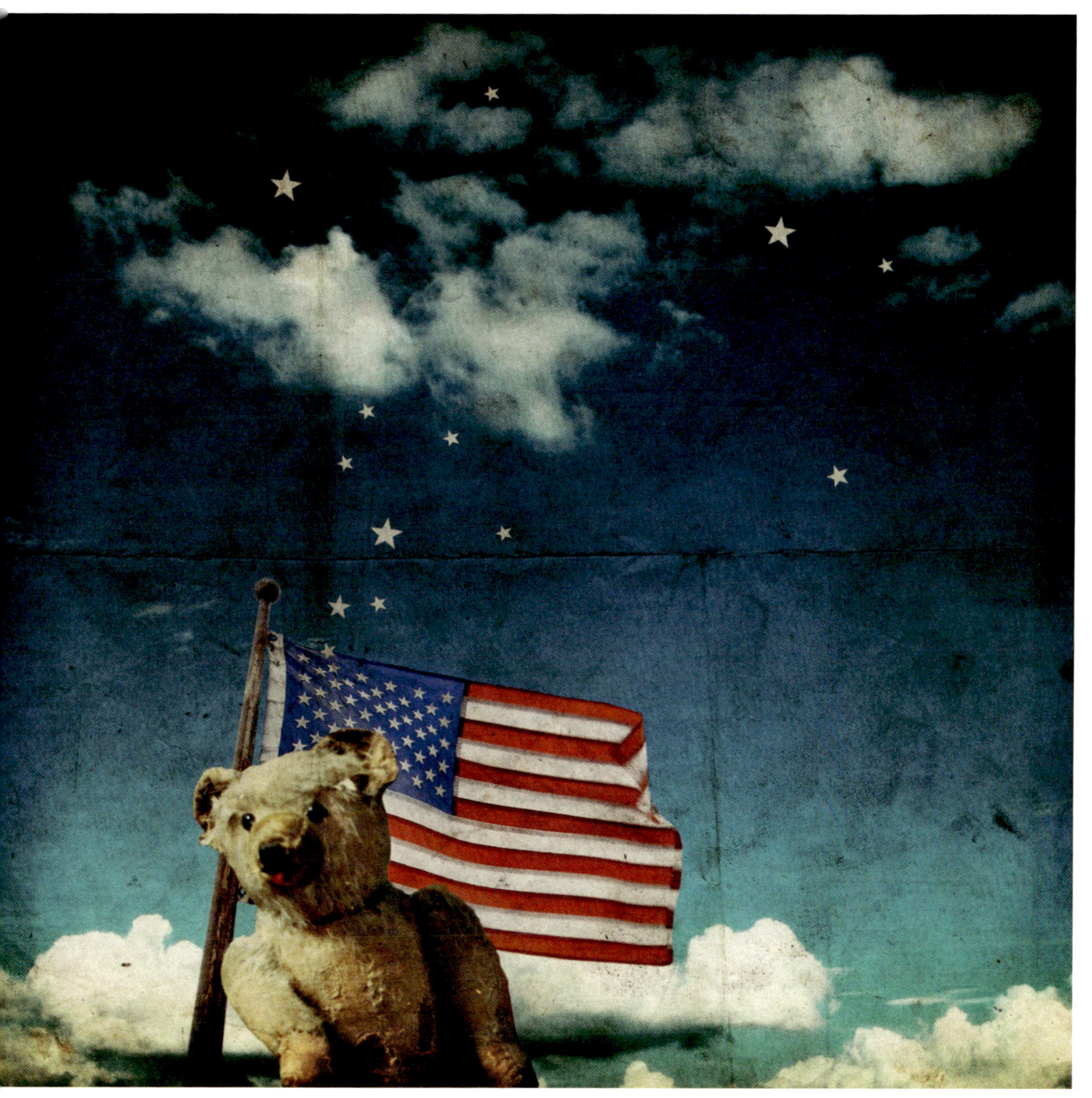

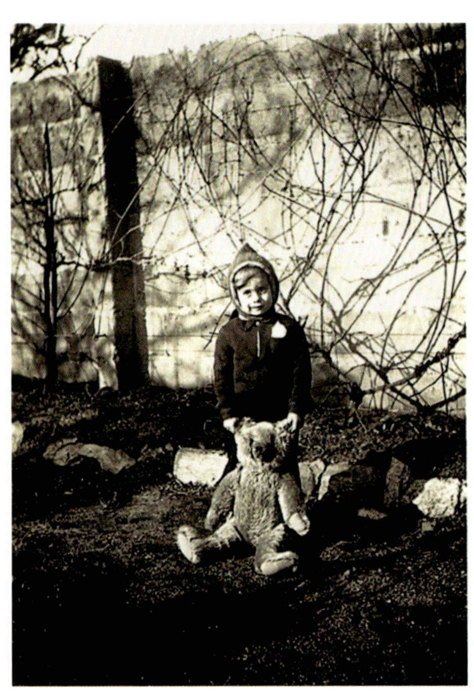

Véronique &
Crosper, 1960s

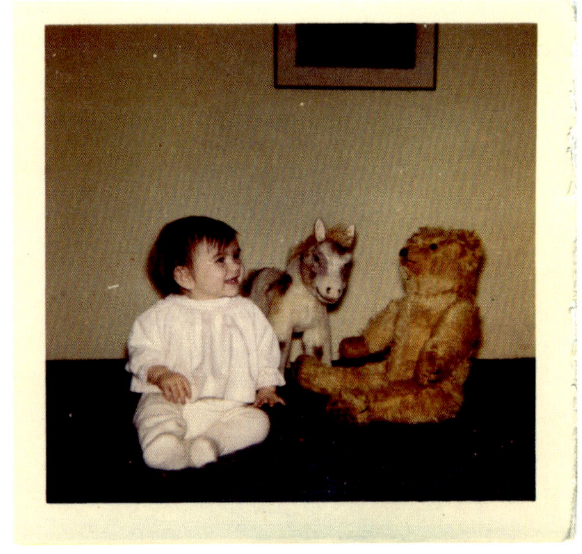

What might Prosper have heard on the radio in the 1940s? Partisan songs, calls to the Resistance on the air waves of the BBC, or Lucienne Delyle singing 'Mon amant de Saint-Jean'?

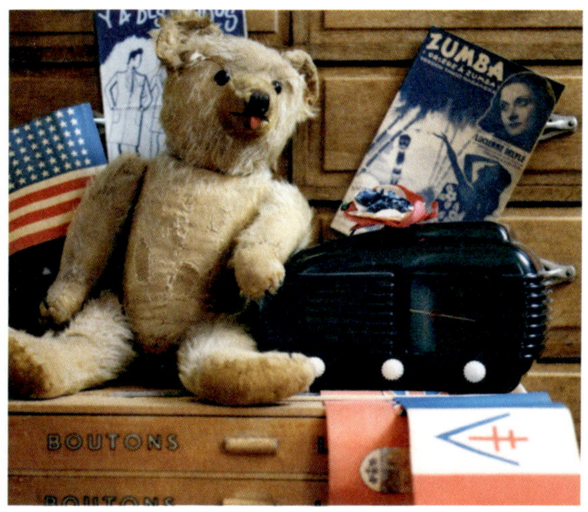

When he was born in 1937 he was the faithful companion of a little boy. He lived through the Second World War and in 1960 was placed in the care of Véronique, the boy's daughter. Father and daughter were companions of the bear.

Sadly the father passed away shortly after the taking of this photograph. Véronique's grief was too immediate – she could not speak of Prosper – and he remained silent.

Michee + Tintin
age: 61
belong to:
Hélène Morey

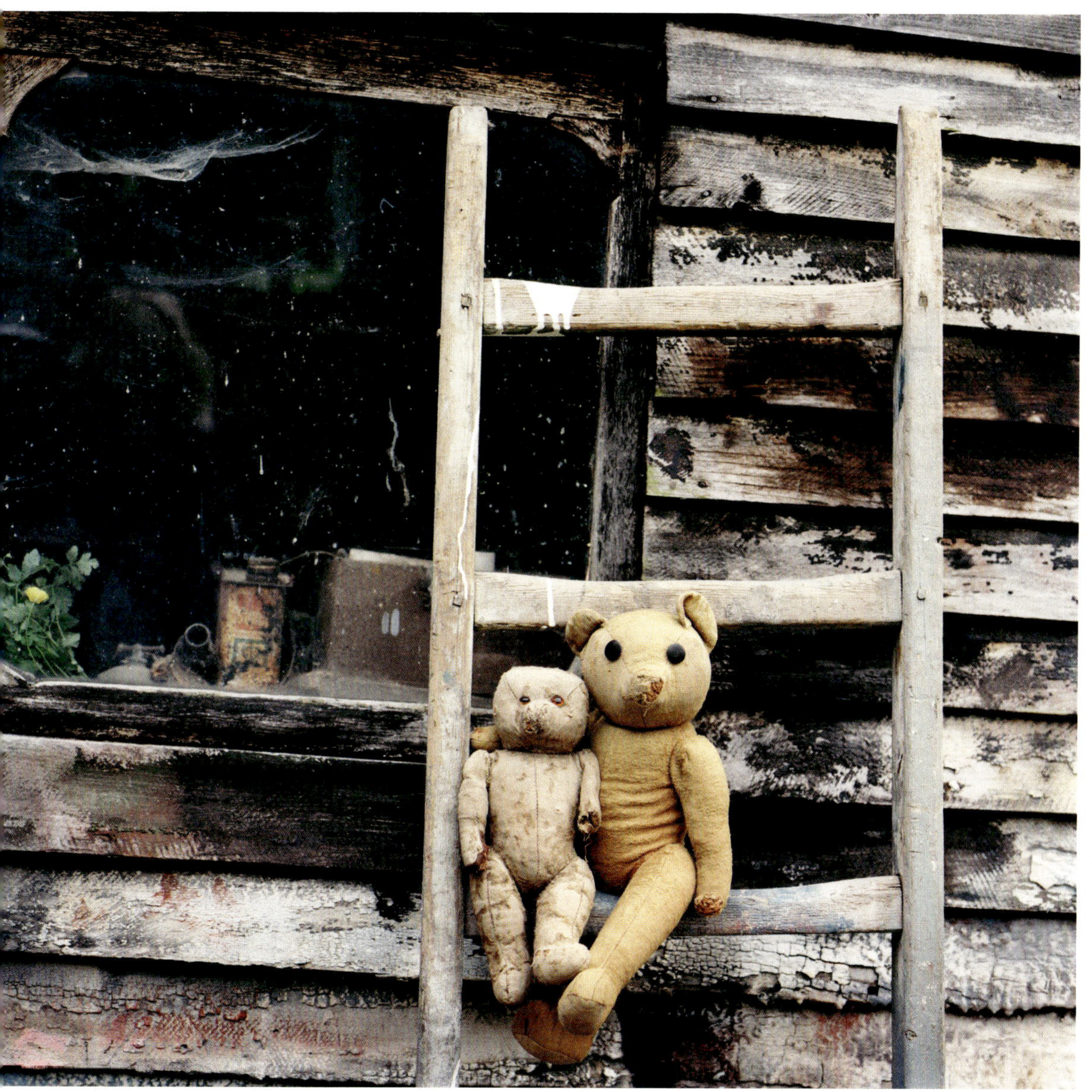

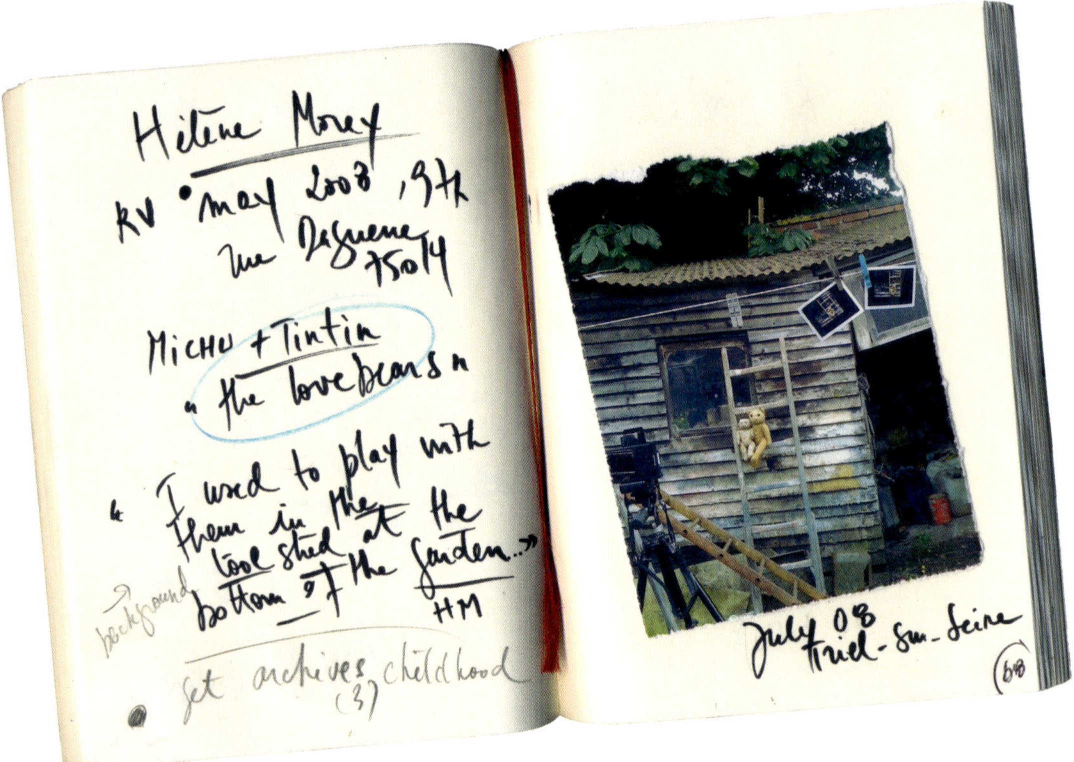

Sylvie, if your story with our friends – stuffed toys, teddies, companions – started with your recovered friend, you have made me see my own as friends. They have never left each other since they first met and they are both wonderful. An unexpected gift from our meeting ...

Hélène de Daguerre

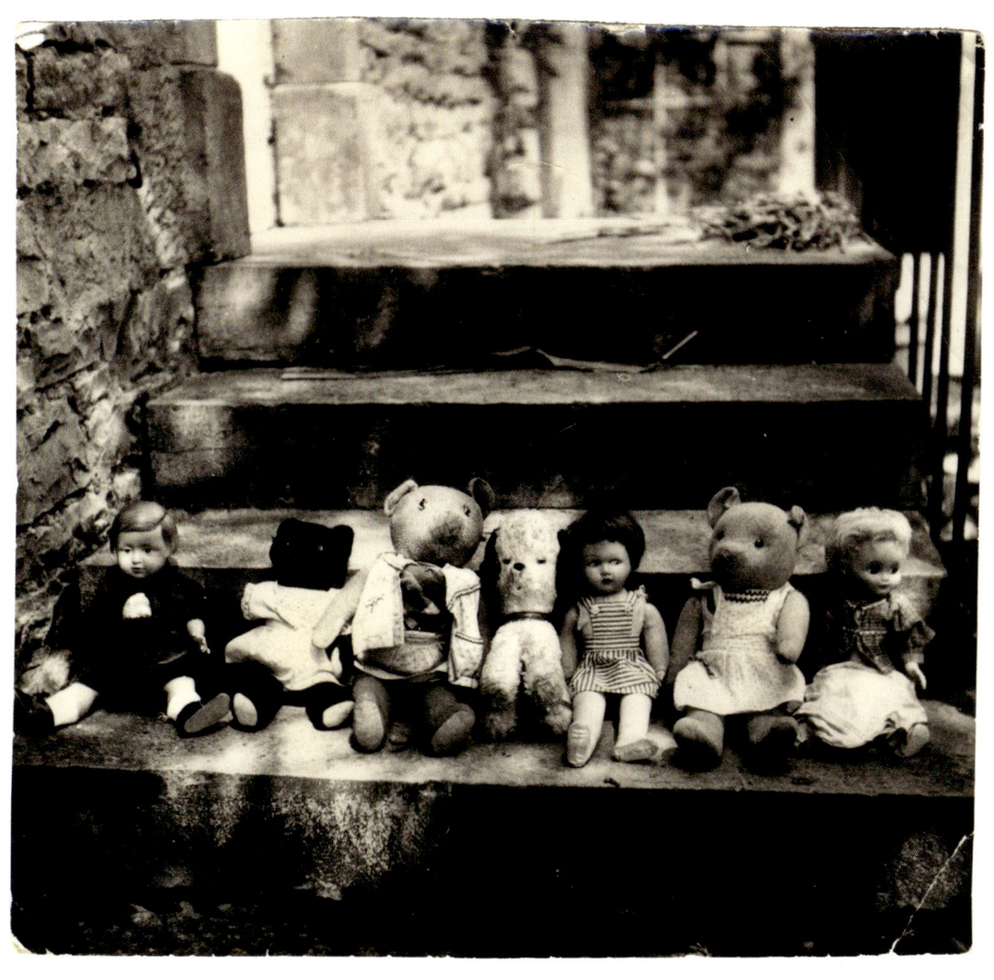

Michuu, Tintin and the others
~ 1960

Beertje

age: 50

belongs to:

Jeroen Haijtink

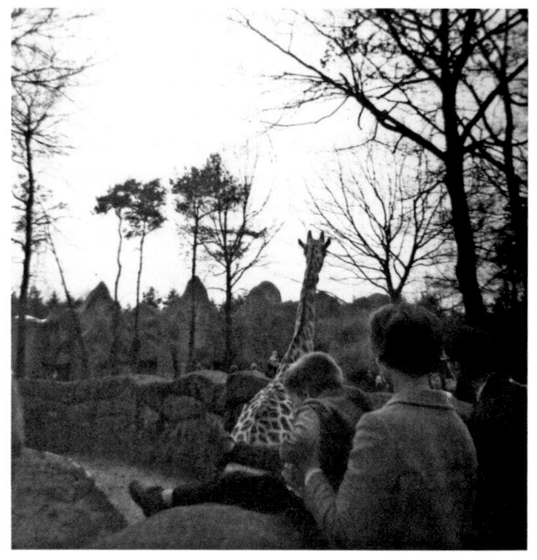

I was given Beertje ('little bear' in Dutch) by my grandparents during my first trip abroad when I was only five months old. Since then I have moved to several different countries, and Beertje has always followed me. These last years Beertje has lived mainly in the suitcase I inherited from my grandfather, alongside the dog my mother knitted and the wooden train my father made.

When I was a young boy living in Belgium, I 'travelled' nearly every Sunday through the jungles of Africa in the Congo Museum in Tervuren. There I met Dr Livingstone and Mr Stanley, discovered indigenous tribes and learned about the apes, elephants, and giraffes, with which I identified because of the physical resemblance (I was already tall as a child and now measure 2.02m).

Years later, I had the opportunity to travel to Africa, thanks to my encounter with Dr Jane Goodall, whose Institute I co-founded in France. Beertje has never made it to Africa, but still imagines his own safari in the suitcase …

Jeroen Haijtink

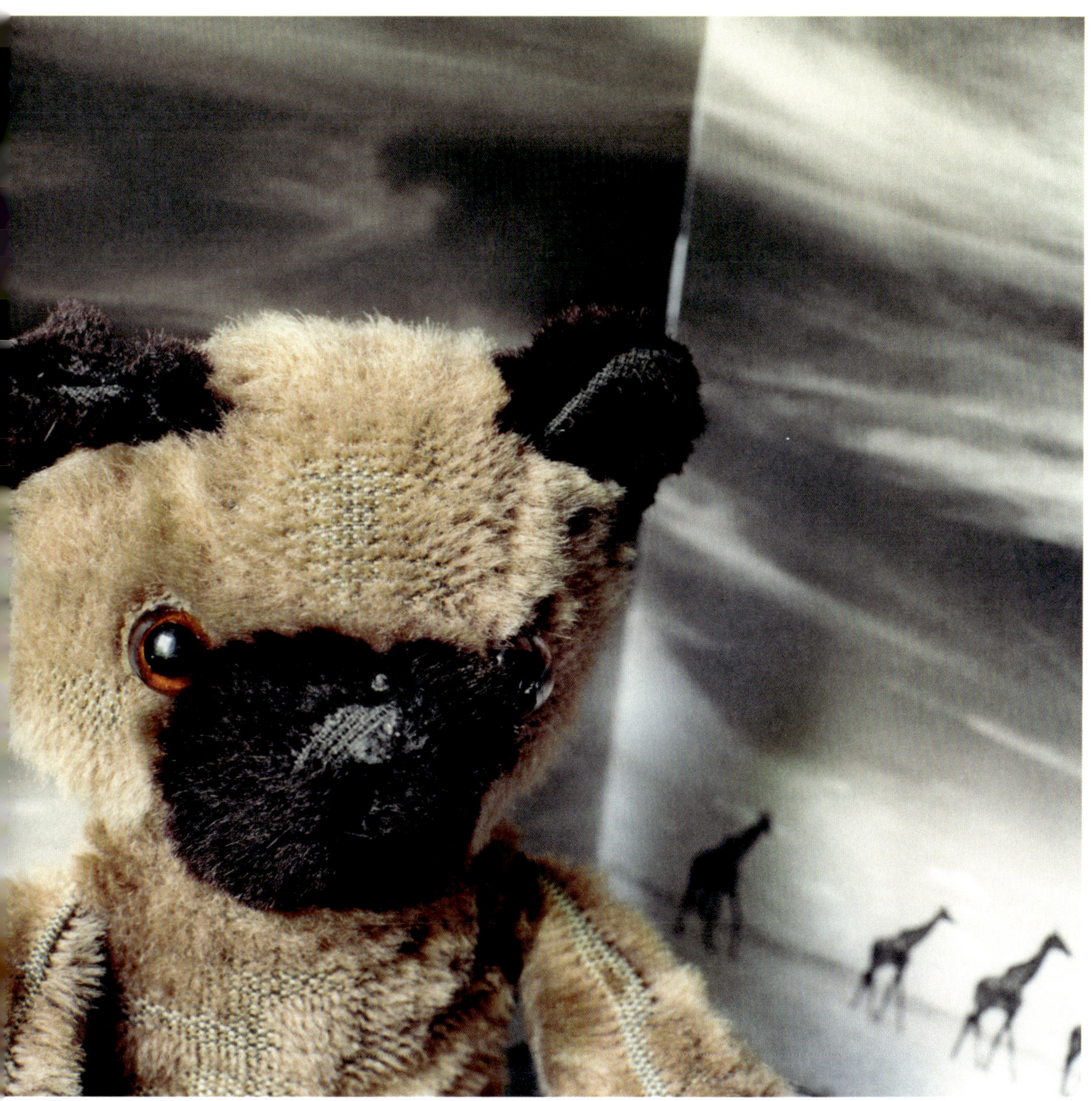

Book
age: 45
belongs to:
Chris Carver

From: Chris Matic
Subject: POOH...
Date: 10 May 2008 15:41:29
To: Sylvie Huet

Sylvie,

I've been having fun telling everyone about your visit to the John K. King bookshop and of your interest in the history of teddy bears, and then in my 'old friend', who is now comfortably back at his retirement home after his brush with stardom! I hope that you are well, it was a wonderful pleasure having you at my home and a very enjoyable afternoon as well. Please take care and watch your mail box.

All the best to you from Detroit.

Yer Pal, Chris

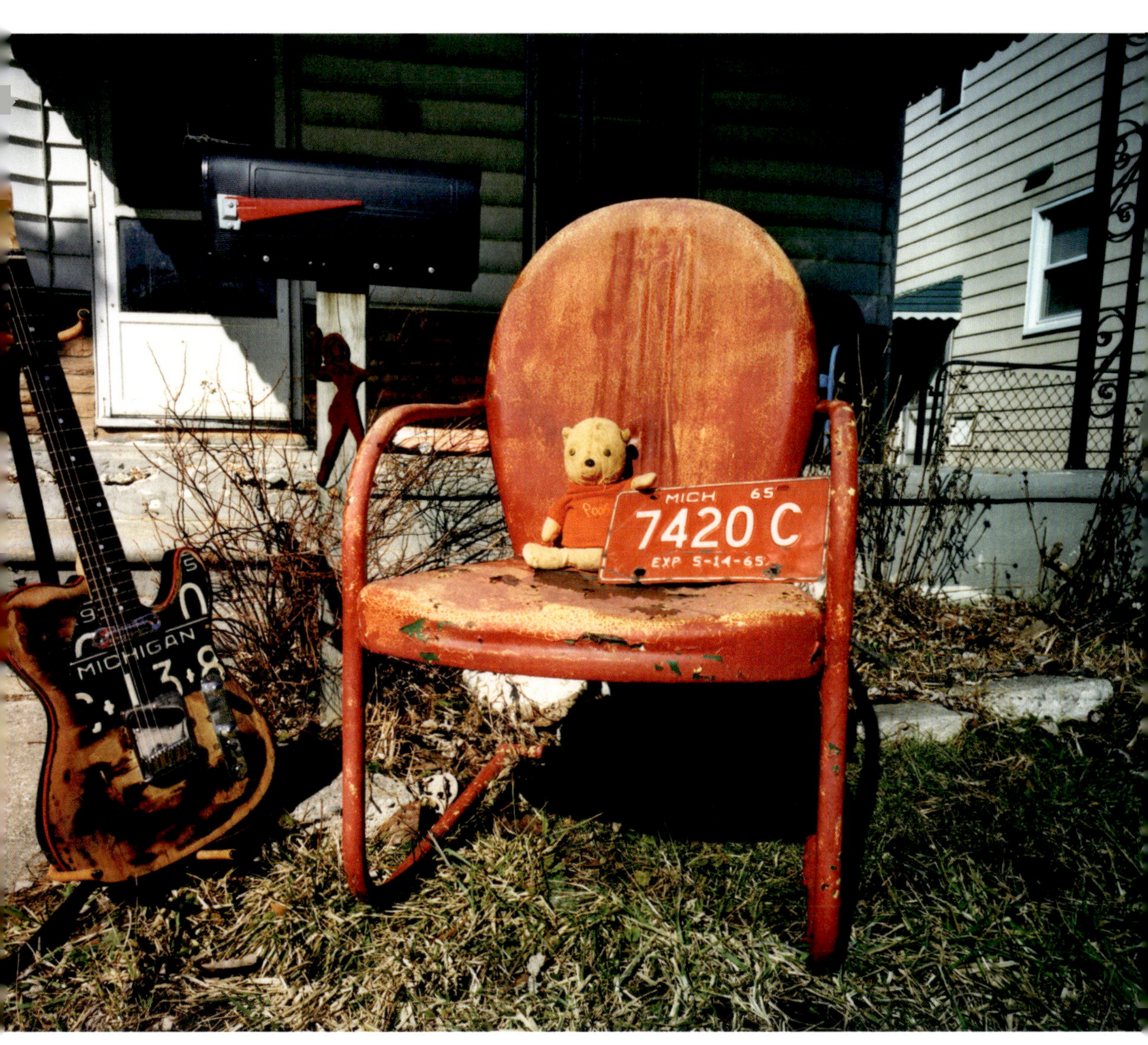
MICH 65
7420 C
EXP 5-14-65
MICHIGAN

Teddy

age: 103

belongs to:

Rhodia Boudelle

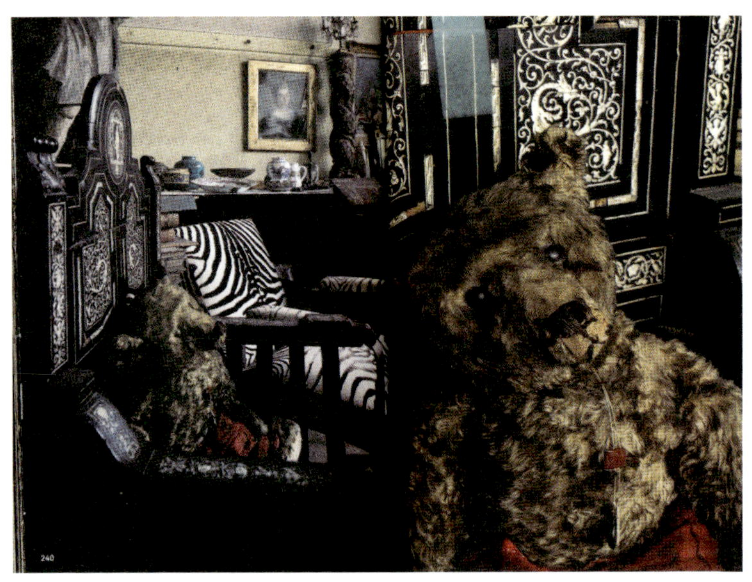

Felice Varini at 18 rue Antoine Bourdelle

When, by chance, I discover the page in the catalogue *Felice Varini at 18 rue Antoine Bourdelle*, my heart starts to race. The photograph was taken in the private apartment of Rhodia, the daughter of the sculptor Antoine Bourdelle. The apartment is within the museum where she was curator from 1949 until her death in 2002. My investigation into 18 rue Antoine Bourdelle begins badly when I learn from a guard that upon the death of Rhodia, "all of her possessions were bequeathed to Emmaüs communities."

"But a bear ..." I insist, saying that often these characters have a special status ... perhaps he still watches over a corner of the museum? Mr. L. patiently asks around, then inquires about my motivation. "If this bear is still here, I would like to meet him."

A few days later I learn from Annie Barbera, from the Department of Documentary Studies, that "the bear is still in her apartment. It is part of the personal belongings of Rhodia Dufet–Bourdelle that have been carefully kept. An 'intimate object' even.".

Even more moving still, is that Rhodia mentions him in her will ...

Rhodia's Teddy bear, 'too big for her
to be able to carry and which she
dragged along by an ear', says Cléopâtre,
wife of sculptor Antoine Bourdelle,
was given to her by Gabriel Thomas,
the founder of the Théâtre des Champs-Élysés
in Paris. Rhodia Dufet-Bourdelle evokes
this in her will: 'This bear has been part
of the life of the Bourdelles since my
childhood, he is a moving witness
who should be respected.'

Annie Barbera

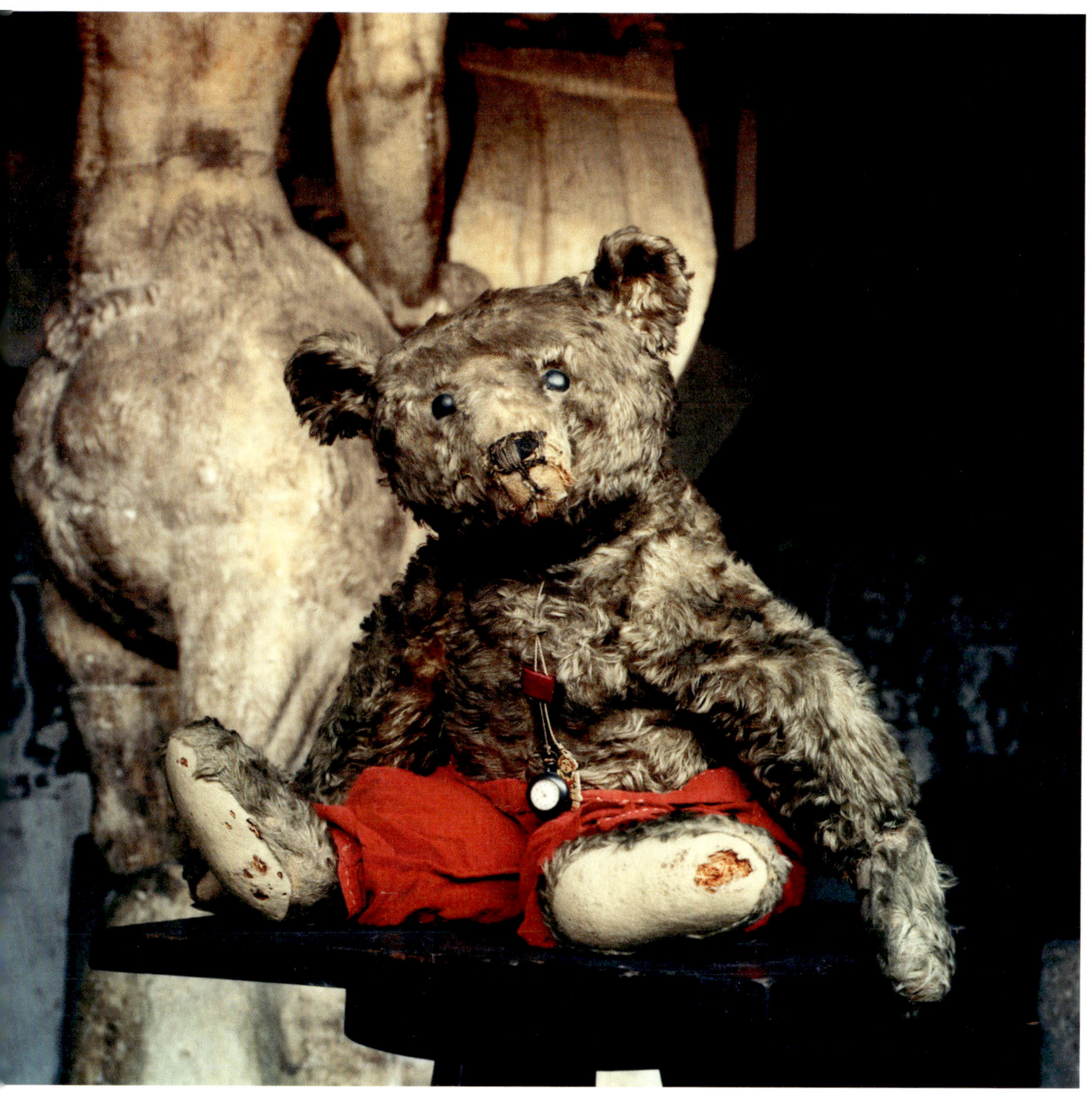

The Golden bear

age: 84

belongs to:

Grandpa George

To begin with he was just
Grandpa George's bear but
once the family saw his
portrait he became a subject
of conversation. He emerged
from the shadows and
became "The golden bear".

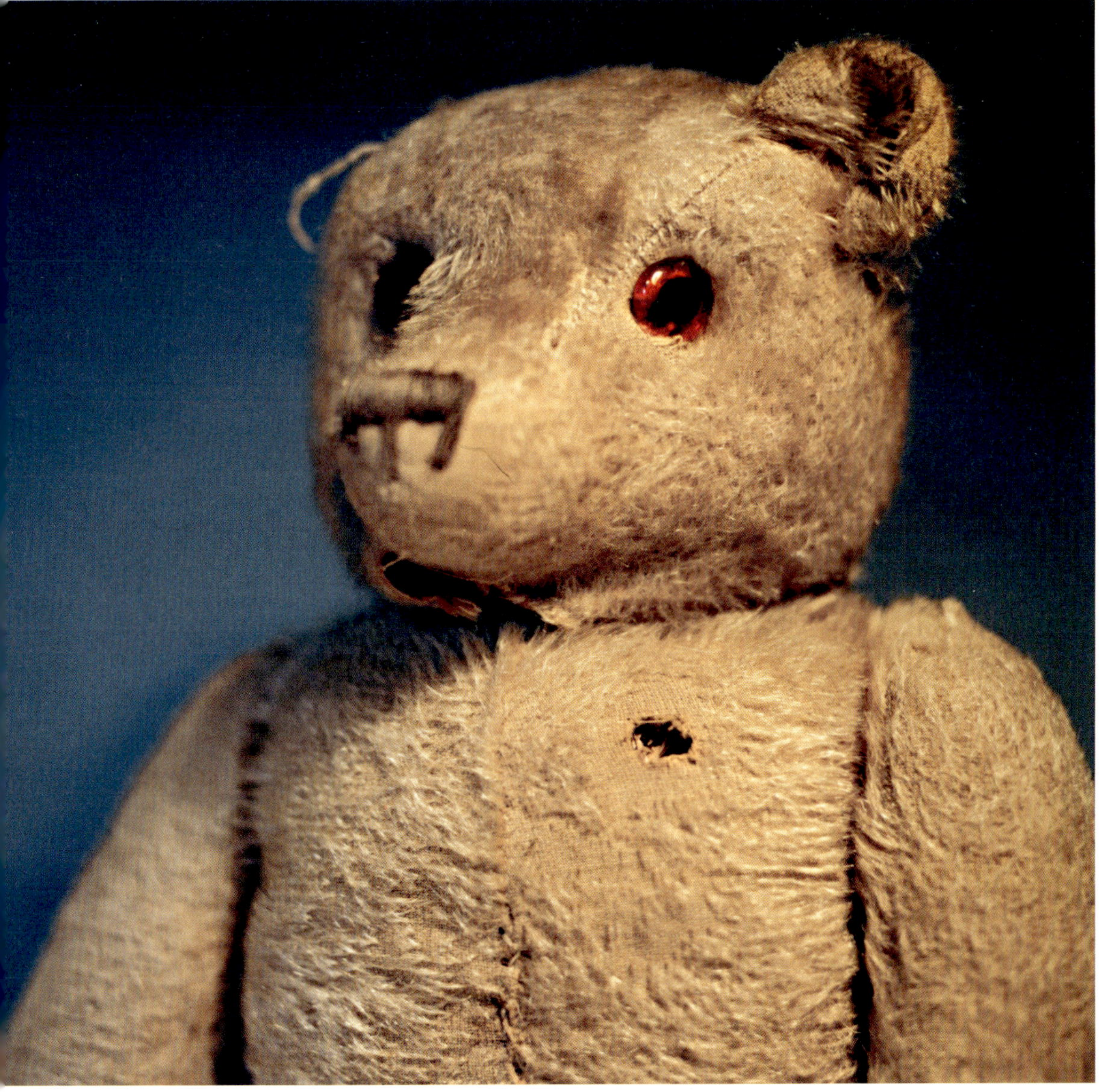

According to Eva,
the hole in the heart
"would be" attributed
to a bullet wound
during Second W. War.!

2emp picture
house of Vandières
where the bear lived.

sept. 09   1 — Eva
contact "Transat"
→ investigation (p. 15)

— mysterious Injured Bear 18/4
Polaroid emulsion transfer
essai 1
otto p.99

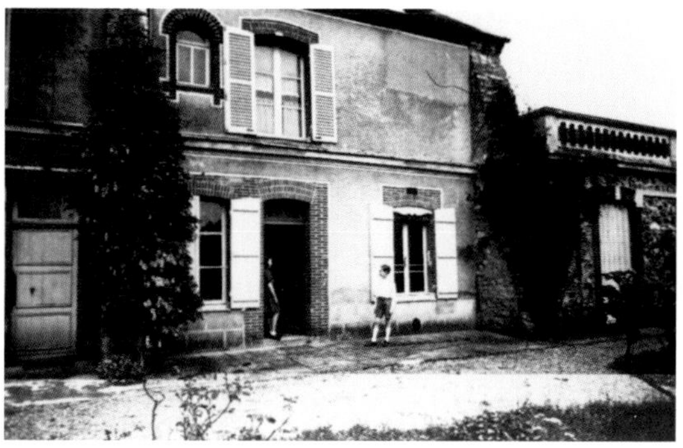

"It was during a dinner that Sylvie talked about a piece of work that she was in the middle of and which revolved around these characters that accompany childhood. She has been rubbing shoulders with them for a long time; it's a story of expressing the soul. Vandières quickly came to mind. There are few houses that, from the nooks to the crannies, and from generation to generation, harbour so many treasures. So this brought me to the teddy of Grandpa Georges, with the injury to his heart, which Bertrand mischieviously attributed to a bullet wound acquired during the Second World War. I believed in that story. Sylvie did to. True or false, it doesn't matter.

Today, his portrait hangs in the living room alongside those of distant ancestors. Thanks to the talent of our visiting artist, he now looks out at us with a slightly stern expression. We're not quite sure what to make of it."

Eva Kempisky

Alan Mearles
age: 51
belongs to:
Grayson Perry

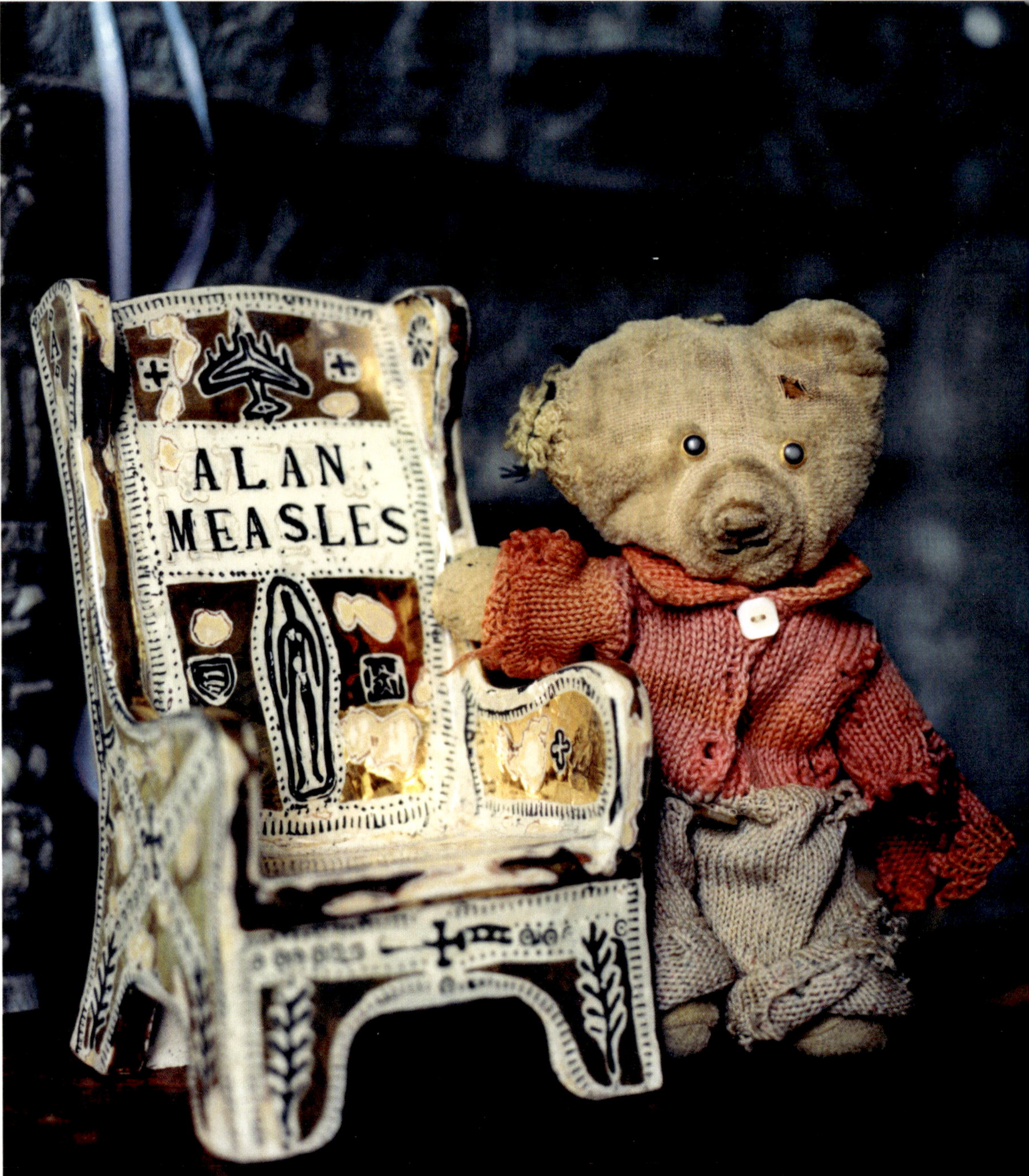
ALAN
MEASLES

"Alan Measles is my fifty-year-old teddy bear. He was the benign dictator of my chilhood imaginary world, where his roles included surrogate father, rebel leader, fighter pilot and undefeated racing driver. I was his bodyguard for he was very precious to me because I had given him all my male qualities of leadership and rebellion. Now he is a guru and living god in my personal cosmology."

Grayson Perry

'Remember!' 'When was it?' 'It comes back to me!'

With every photograph an investigation would start.
Photographing a bear was like entering a family secret.

I thank every bear owner for these unforseen moments.

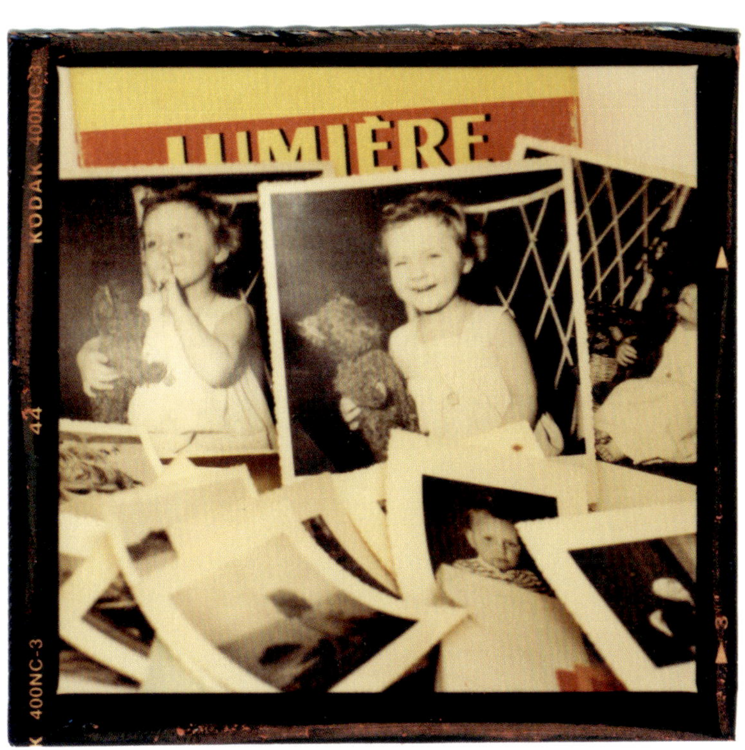

LUMIÈRE

Notes and credits

page 5
À la guerre comme à la guerre,
Tomi Ungerer, éditions La Nuée Bleue 1991,
L'école des loisirs, 2002.

page 22
background: table-mat / Créations Isaac,
Paris.

page 28
Michka, Marie Colmont, 1941.

page 39 / 135
©Jules Maillard.

page 52
Magnus, Sylvie Germain, éditions Albin
Michel, 2005. Excerpt translated DLP.

page 62
Mes parents, Hervé Guibert, éditions
Gallimard, 1986. Excerpt translated DLP.

page 63
background: reproduction from
Photographies, Christine Guibert ©Hervé
Guibert, Gallimard, 1993.

page 90
©Tomi Ungerer, Musée Tomi Ungerer –
Centre International de l'Illustration.

page 91
Otto, autobiographie d'un ours en peluche,
Tomi Ungerer, Diogenes Verlag, 1999.

page 101
The Fashion World of Jean Paul Gaultier
'From the Sidewalk to the Catwalk'
(2011-2015): International tour initiated
by Nathalie Bondil, Musée des beaux-arts,
Montréal, curated by Thierry-Maxime
Loriot. Exhibition catalogue: éditions
Musée des beaux arts / La Martinière,
Paris, 2011.

page 102 / 103
text ©Jean Paul Gaultier from
The Fashion World of Jean Paul Gaultier
(first published in ACTUEL, Paris, 1990).
Prototype chest of drawers ©Jean Paul
Gaultier.

page 130
www.barbara-wahnemuehl.de

page 147
background: ©Nick Brandt, *L'Afrique au
crépuscule*, La Martinière, 2009.
www.biglife.org

page 154
©André Morin. Reproduction from
Felice Varini au 18 rue Antoine Bourdelle,
éditions Xavier Barral, 2006.

page 167
The Tomb of the Unknown Craftsman,
Grayson Perry, The British Museum
Press, 2011.

Acknowledgements

Thanks for having opened doors:
Annie Barbera and Amélie Simier,
musée Antoine Bourdelle, Paris;
Christine Guibert / Hervé Guibert;
Aria Ungerer / Tomi Ungerer; Thérèse
Willer, Musée Tomi Ungerer-Centre
International de l'Illustration,
Strasbourg; Jelka Music / Jean Paul
Gaultier; Thierry-Maxime Loriot and
Arkitektur-Och Design Centrum,
Stockholm; Jeroen Haijtink and
Monica Lieschke, Jane Goodall
Institute; Charlotte Tory, Grayson
Perry's assistant.

Thanks to: Anne-Laurence Dalloz,
Eva Kempisky, Claire Perenchio,
Hélène & Caso.

Special thanks: to my parents;
to Jörg Hoyer and Dieter; to Caroline
Warhurst and Dewi Lewis for their
friendly look on this eccentric project;
to Hahnemühle for providing fine art
paper; to Françoise Bourhis / Kodak
for supporting film costs; and to
Hervé Caté / Labo Imaginoir, for his
involvement in *A Story of Bears*.

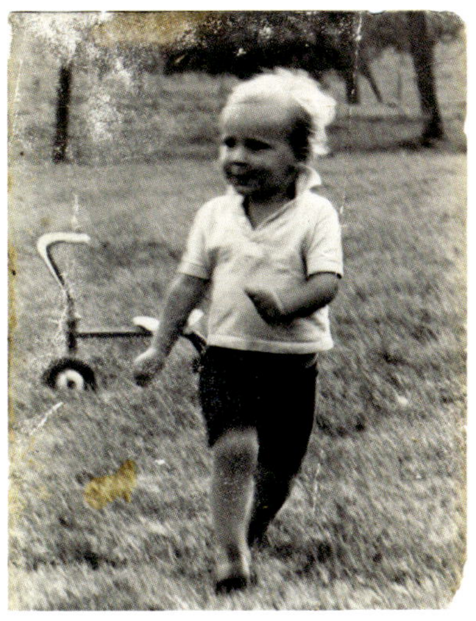

First published in the UK in 2014 by

Dewi Lewis Publishing
8 Broomfield Road
Heaton Moor
Stockport SK4 4ND
England

www.dewilewispublishing.com

photographs: Sylvie Huet
texts: Sylvie Huet and bear owners
references: as credited on p.170
archive images: courtesy of the families
for this edition: Dewi Lewis Publishing

ISBN: 978-1-907893-59-9

Design: Caroline Warhurst & Sylvie Huet
Print: EBS, Verona, Italy